BETWEEN THE DEVIL & THE DEEP BLUE BAY

San Francisco Bay continually faces the dilemma of conflicting private and public interests. The Bay is our greatest natural resource, influencing our climate, sustaining wildlife and vegetation, providing beauty and recreation for those who live near its shores. But, with continuing urbanization, industrialization and added population pressures, the Bay is also a desirable source of revenue to subdivision developers, freeway planners, garbage dumpers and municipal governments seeking added land for industrial sites to add to their tax rolls.

This book puts the battle for the Bay in perspective: historically, politically, economically, legally. Against the story of those who have plundered, destroyed and filled the Bay since the beginnings of San Francisco, it sets the work of conservation-minded private citizens and politicians who are working constructively to save the Bay.

It is already too late to correct the mistakes caused by a century of greed, shortsightedness and apathy. BETWEEN THE DEVIL AND THE DEEP BLUE BAY is a warning and a plea for action—now—before the process of destruction of San Francisco Bay is irreversible.

PREVIOUS BOOKS BY HAROLD GILLIAM

San Francisco Bay
The Face of San Francisco
Island in Time: The Pt. Reyes Peninsula
Weather of the San Francisco Bay Region
San Francisco: City at The Golden Gate, *with Ann Gilliam*
American Heritage Book of Natural Wonders, *Pacific Coast Section*
The Natural World of San Francisco

BETWEEN  THE DEEP
THE DEVIL BLUE BAY

THE STRUGGLE TO SAVE SAN FRANCISCO BAY

BY HAROLD GILLIAM
CHRONICLE BOOKS/SAN FRANCISCO

Dedicated to the
Save San Francisco Bay Association
P.O. Box 925
Berkeley, California 94701

YOU always remember the first time you saw San Fran-cisco Bay. It comes back to you in later years with vivid intensity: the sudden, breath-taking impact of that initial moment when the great Bay was first spread out before you, fresh and new and shining.

. . . You may have seen it first from the air or from one of its highway approaches or from the deck of the Oakland ferry at sundown, when the water around you was luminous with crimson fire and vertical patterns of lights glowed from the darkening towers of San Francisco. Then, suddenly, no matter what your age, you were young, and the Bay around you and the city beyond it were the future, full of great and glowing promise.

At that moment, whenever it may have been, you became a member of that company of explorers, pioneers, Argon-auts, and empire builders who came to this edge of the New World when the land was young and, like you, felt a sudden blaze of exhilaration.

— San Francisco Bay

5

PREFACE

This book is in some ways a sequel to *San Francisco Bay*. In that volume, first published in 1957, the author described the filling of the Bay and wrote: "The current rapid encroachment of residential subdivisions and industrial sites raises a serious question about the Bay's future . . . For most of the Bay to be replaced by mile after mile of solidly-built-up suburbs would be to eliminate the area's greatest natural advantage."

In the following decade ten square miles of the Bay were "reclaimed." The Army Corps of Engineers warned that if filling and diking continued at the same rate as in the past the Bay would be reduced to a channel within 100 years.

This book is concerned with what happened in that decade and with prospects for the Bay's future. Its major premise is that the crisis provides an unprecedented opportunity, calling attention not only to the threat to the Bay's existence but also to its unfulfilled possibilities.

Along most of the 276 miles of shoreline, communities have turned their backs on the Bay, and it has become inaccessible and unattractive. Remove the dumps that now clutter its shoreline, eliminate the sewage that pollutes its waters, make it accessible to the public at all points, and it could become the center and core of urban and suburban living. There would be ample space along the shores for essential water-related industrial and commercial activities, for marinas, swimming beaches, fishing piers, parks, Bay museums, and marshes vital to fish and wildlife.

Shoreline communities could once again face the Bay, look out across its shining surface from parks and landscaped waterfronts, and make use of boat travel as public transportation for both business and pleasure. In the coming age of automation, as American ways of life become increasingly oriented toward the new leisure, the Bay Area will be uniquely equipped to develop new patterns of living centered around water-based recreation.

It is particularly important, in this time of urban troubles, that many of the blighted inner-city areas of this region are located near the Bay's shores. Developing the recreational potentialities of the shoreline in these districts will open the walls of the slums and ghettos to the Bay and should be the first order of business in shoreline development.

The San Francisco Bay Plan, as devised over a three-year period by the Bay Conservation and Development Commission and summarized later in these pages, has been described in its preliminary form by Dr. Leslie Carbert, former State Planning Officer, as "one of the most exciting and unique planning documents in modern American experience." It is not a perfect or finished document, but it is the first major step anywhere in the United States toward an enforceable regional plan embracing several counties and dozens of cities. If the plan is strengthened rather than weakened by the Legislature, it promises to become a catalyst, stimulating efforts here and elsewhere to transform the chaos of metropolitan sprawl into rational, comprehensive planning for an orderly, efficient, beautiful and humane environment.

More than a century ago, when the Golden Gate was the entrance to El Dorado, San Francisco Bay became a worldwide symbol of opportunity and high promise. Now, in a time of environmental crisis, it may once again be the destiny of this Bay to play that historic role.

10

ACKNOWLEDGEMENTS

The author is deeply indebted to dozens of Bay Area residents who have helped with the preparation of this book both directly and indirectly. Unfortunately only a few of them can be listed here.

Among them are Professor Francis P. Felice of the University of San Francisco, who many years ago first called my attention to the shrinkage of the Bay and its significance; David Brower of the Sierra Club, who conceived the idea of this book; Mel Scott, whose penetrating study *The Future of San Francisco Bay,* published by the Institute of Governmental Studies at the University of California, was a principal source document; Executive Director Joseph E. Bodovitz, Deputy Director Alvin H. Baum Jr., and the staff of the Bay Conservation and Development Commission for answering innumerable requests for information and for permission to use BCDC photographs, maps and other materials; those indefatigable and invaluable Bay Area civic leaders, Mrs. Morse Erskine, Mrs. Clark Kerr, Mrs. Donald McLaughlin, Mrs. Charles Gulick, Mrs. Ralph Jacobson; the Save San Francisco Bay Association (P.O. Box 925, Berkeley 94701); William Penn Mott, Jr., past president, and William Siri, current president of that association; Laurel Raynolds for her excellent documentary film, "San Francisco Bay''; marine biologist Joel Gustavson; George F. Collins and Doris L. Leonard of Conservation Associates; Warren Lindquist, Robert Cranmer and their colleagues of Westbay Community Associates.

Doubtless they would not all agree completely with the viewpoints presented here and are not to be held responsible for any errors of fact or aberrations of opinion.

Thanks are also due to Doubleday & Company for permission to reprint excerpts from *San Francisco Bay* and to the editors of *The San Francisco Chronicle* for the assignment that enabled me to cover the Bay as part of my regular duties.

CONTENTS

13

THIS is the place where the Pacific, eternally assaulting the land, has breached the thousand-mile mountain barrier at the western edge of the continent. Its rhythmic tides surge between the dark red cliffs on either side of the strait, flood the long basin in the coastal hills, and cleave through the inner rim of mountains into the heart of the Central Valley.

Out of this violent meeting of land and sea was born the Bay named for St. Francis of Assisi.

Long rolling combers from the ocean explode into geysers of spray on its headlands. Giant winds roar through its entrance, bringing the life-giving moisture of the sea to the arid inner valleys, creating the great summer fogs which pour through the strait in massive flowing forms like living glaciers.

This is the incomparable harbor that remained hidden behind the mountain wall for more than two centuries while scores of navigators sailed along the coast without sighting its entrance.

This is the Bay that was the focal point of the greatest treasure hunt in history when the modern Argonauts sailed their thousand ships here and set out for gold.

And this is the mountain-bordered inland sea which became the nerve center of a western empire, rimmed by a dozen cities, harboring ships and planes from around the world. Yet its waves still wash remote shores where deer and beaver and mink come to the water's edge, where sea lions roar, where great flocks of birds stop off in their long migrations down the flyways of the hemisphere.

The Bay is two trillion gallons of salt water covering four hundred square miles. One of the great ports of the earth, it contains the nation's largest naval base and includes a number of subsidiary bays, including Richardson, San Pablo, and Suisun. It is the only outlet to the sea for the sixty-thousand-square-mile Central Valley of California; into it flow the waters of sixteen rivers.

On the wild shores, life-giving marshlands

It encloses ten islands and is spanned by the world's greatest bridges. Its opaque surface hides swarming colonies of marine life from shrimps to sharks, and its channels carry currents mightier than the continent's biggest rivers.

It is a mirror of the sky, reflecting the sun, the gray summer fogs and white clouds, the crimson and purple twilight, the jeweled amber lamps of its long arching bridges, the shimmer of moonrise above the eastern mountains.

It tempers the weather; affects the winds, fogs and rains that move across its surface; influences the crops and industries around it; and shapes in countless ways the lives of four million people who live and work on its shores.

— San Francisco Bay

On the urban shores, water-oriented living.

*Into these portals,
a procession of ships*

The call of the mast, the lure of the wilds

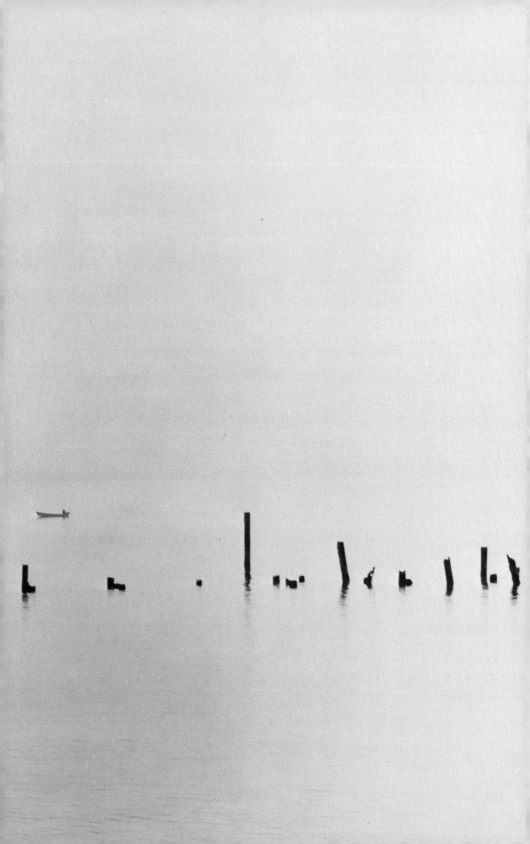

1/ THIS JEWELLED SURFACE

TO the yachtsman San Francisco Bay is weekend release from workday routine; it is the excitement of a regatta, with full canvas and flying spray and the sails of half a hundred vessels against the blue water. It is the smell of salt wind and the flight of a gull and the froth of whitecaps. It is loafing in the sun as the boat rises and falls on the swells. It is leisurely exploration of winding channels and shorelines in a maze of Delta islands. It is the kind of recreation and renewal that comes from first-hand contact with the elements — with the sun and fog and rising tide, with the roaring winds and flowing waters.

To a bar pilot or tugmaster or the Marine Exchange lookout on the end of Pier 45 near Fisherman's Wharf, the Bay is a daily procession of ships: the freighters of all the earth's seafaring nations sailing in through the Golden Gate; the long low tankers with crude oil from the fields of the San Joaquin or the wells of tropical Sumatra; the majestic passenger liners like great floating cities — the *Lurline* from Honolulu, or the *President Cleveland* returning from Yokohama, or the giant white *Oriana* from London.

To the sportsman the Bay is a cold clear fall morning in a duck blind, the rewarding sight of a flock of mallards in

ragged V-formation, their feathers pink in the morning sun; to the fisherman in a skiff off The Brothers lighthouse it is the sudden knot of excitement that comes with a tug on a line and a roll of the boat as a big striped bass hits the bait.

To the resident of Telegraph Hill or Pacific Heights or Berkeley or Sausalito, or any of the rim of hills that circle this water for 100 miles, it is the refreshment of a cool breeze on a hot day; it is a gargantuan stage for the weather, for the gray clouds trailing long banners of rain, for floods of summer fog that flow through the Golden Gate and over the Bay's hills in massive cascades; it is the changing play of light on a surface that reflects the patterns of illumination and shade from low-flying cumulus clouds or wisps of fog; it is a sunset spectrum of golds and pinks and reds and purples merging into gray and, finally, a gulf of black surrounded by the constellations of cities along the far shores.

To the marine biologist the Bay is a rich repository of estuarine life from larvae to clams to crabs to leaping salmon; it is also a potential source of food supply for the future millions of people who will live in the megalopolis around its shores.

To the bird enthusiast the Bay is home for millions of resident waterfowl and for migratory flocks on the Pacific Flyway; it is a long line of a hundred cormorants abreast skimming the surface between Brooks Island and the Golden Gate; it is the wheeling flight of a thousand avocets swooping into the marshes of Bay Farm Island on the ebb tide; it is the nesting area of a colony of Caspian terns on the salt ponds at Dumbarton Point; it is a russet-colored Virginia rail swimming among the golden salicornia grasses in a marsh near Alviso; it is a single white egret curving in parabolic flight toward a roosting place on Marin Island.

27

"Reclaiming" the Bay

But if San Francisco Bay means to some people taut sails and salt spray, or a parade of ships, or the wonder of wildlife, it means something quite different to other people.

To many a developer and land speculator the Bay is real estate to be filled with dirt and covered with houses and shopping centers and factories.

To some city and county planning officials the Bay offers the opportunity seldom available to members of the profession — the chance to create new communities, a blank space on the drawing board to be filled in with attractive pictures of subdivisions or "industrial parks."

To highway engineers the Bay is an ideal place to build freeways, without the onerous problems of routing through established communities and fighting the opposition of residents.

To local sanitation officials and garbage disposal contractors, who must dispose of thousands of tons of wastes daily, the Bay makes an ideal garbage dump or cesspool.

Around these shores the dump trucks and bulldozers are busy hauling refuse to the water's edge, gouging the bayside hills to fill the shoreline indentations and embayments, converting open water to dry land for more dreary developments of the kind that stretch endlessly around many another U. S. city in all directions.

In the past few years these waters have become the high stakes of a battle being waged on many fronts — political, economic, legal, educational — between those who would destroy large parts of the Bay by filling and those who would defend it as open water, as the region's greatest natural resource, as a superb opportunity for recreation, as a source of beauty and inspiration and breathing space for the supercrowded Bay Area of the future.

2 / A BILLION YEARS
AT BAY FARM ISLAND

IN San Francisco the fog still enveloped the city, but at Bay Farm Island, south of Alameda, the morning sun was gleaming from the sandy beaches and from the winding channels of the marshes, flooded by a high tide. As you gazed out across the Bay, the surface was calm and glassy. The only sounds you could hear were a far-off train whistle and the distant clatter of tractors plowing an anachronistic celery field across the "island" — actually a peninsula.

Out at the Golden Gate, the currents had begun to flow westward, drawn by the sinking ocean, and now along these shores the waters began to ebb slowly. In a thousand channels among the reeds and tules and the salicornia marshes the water was moving, bending the grasses that had been engulfed by the high tide.

The turning of the tide is a momentous event on all the shores of the Bay. On their loafing grounds along the upper shores of Bay Farm Island and the beaches of Alameda, the flocks of shore birds that had been resting somnolently began to stir.

A small western sandpiper quickly fluttered into the air, and almost simultaneously the entire flock rose with him. Other flocks rose a moment later, and soon legions of the sparrow-sized birds flashed through the sky and settled on a sandy flat newly exposed by the ebb.

They ran with darting movements so quick that you could

barely discern the motion of their short legs, and they seemed to be scooting on wheels. Hungrily they probed the glis-
tening margin of the sand with their stubby bills for succu-
lent crustaceans.

After probing one patch of sand, the small birds suddenly rose as a unit into the air and wheeled in arcs down the
beach, almost disappearing as they banked on a turn and
their gray backs blended with the sky, then flashing brilliant-
ly as they turned again and the white undersurfaces of their
wings caught the sunlight.

Eight big long-billed curlews swooped down in formation
among the smaller sandpipers and began to probe the sand
with their incredibly elongated down-curved bills. Sand organisms that can escape the shallow probing of the sandpipers by digging deeper cannot evade the scythe-like beaks
of these birds, reaching lengths of six or seven inches.

Then the curlews took off again down the beach, whistling their alarm, a haunting cry that reminds you of a verse
of Tennyson:

'Tis the place, and all around it, as of old, the curlews call
Dreary gleams about the moorland flying over
Locksley Hall ...

Just offshore a bird the size of a small gull beat his wings
rapidly, hovering over one spot, peering down at the water.
Then he plummeted to the surface with a massive splash and
rose into the air again, having speared a delectable morsel.

From his manner of flying, his forked tail, and his red
bill, you were able to identify him readily: he was a Caspian
tern, a member of a tribe of long-distance migrants. Some
of his relatives annually make a round trip from the Arctic
to the Antarctic.

As the water continued to drain off the tide flats, leaving

acres of gleaming wet sand, the shorebird activity increased. There were long-legged willets and marbled godwits, plovers and kildeers and immense flocks of avocets with long up-turned bills and zigzag black-and-white stripes that flashed gaudily as they flew by.

A helicopter clattered noisily overhead, and the birds rose from the feeding grounds by the thousands. The sky was filled with the interlocking spirals of wheeling masses of flocks flying in cross directions, scintillating in the sun, whirling about a central axis or riding the currents down to the sand again.

Behind them was a spectacular backdrop — the Berkeley hills rising in undulating folds to the skyline, the high white buildings of downtown Oakland, the giant gray shape of an aircraft carrier at the Alameda naval base, the long sweep-ing arcs of the Bay Bridge, and the skyscrapers of San Fran-cisco rising into the gray mists like a mirage on the far shore.

For a hundred yards offshore, as the tide ebbed to an ex-treme low, the birds raced and probed and wheeled over the wet sands. The water ran off in streaks and shallow streams, leaving alternating channels and flattened ridges that re-flected the sun in patterns of dazzling light.

As you watched the marshland you discerned, emerging from the marsh, a lumbering bear of a man who seemed to be an indigenous element of the natural scene. With a beard and a trident he would have made a convincing tideland Neptune. He had evidently lived so long in this place that it was hard to tell where the marsh left off and the man began. Wisps of marsh plants and soil clung to his clothes and skin and formed an aromatic salty aureole.

This was Lehi Torrey, adventurer, hedgehopping flyer,

tugboat skipper, philosoper, Thoreau of the marshlands. He was willing to tell you the story of his 500-year-old Chinese junk, but it soon became evident that his consuming interest was in the marsh itself, several hundred acres of grasses, winding channels, sand flats, and open water. He scooped up a fistful of mud and waved it in front of you. "This is the most heavily-populated part of the earth! In one cubic inch of tideland mud there are 40,000 living organisms!"

He went on to tell you about the chain of life that makes tidelands like this vital to the wildlife of all of San Francisco Bay, to the flocks of migrating birds and the fish prized by anglers.

He pulled up an old board from the mud, pointed to the swarming life beneath as if he were unearthing a treasure of crown jewels. He picked up a few hopping mites that he described as brine shrimp, morsels as delectable to birds and fish as their larger cousins are to humans.

But his greatest enthusiasm was reserved for a little animal called the teredo, the shipworm with a voracious appetite for pier pilings and the hulls of wooden vessels. His story of the life cycle of the teredo was narrated with all the excitement and humor of a Disney documentary.

Suddenly you had the feeling that you were looking at two ends of a scale representing a billion years. It may have been in some similar marsh that our remote forebears first emerged from the Paleozoic waters and began the long, painful ascent.

It occurred to you that this tideland marsh, with its rhythmic flooding and ebbing waters, its teeming forms of life, its spawning fish, and its great wheeling flocks of shore birds was not only an area of austere natural beauty in the midst of a crowded urban area; it was a lens providing a view out of our cranny of space and time into the labyrinthine reaches of organic evolution, the slow processes by which life evolved from the protoplasmic mud to the flight of the marsh birds and the cities on these shores.

Yet even these cities were not the ultimate result of the evolutionary process but only some intermediate stage on the way to an unknowable destination, and the species in the cities may be as primitive, in relation to future forms of life, as the creatures in this mud seem to us.

When you tuned in on Lehi again, you realized that he was not talking biology now but was elaborating on the future of this marsh. His story was alarming: Alameda city officials had approved of a developer's plan to wipe out the marsh by filling it for a subdivision. It apparently had not occurred to them that the area might be worth far less as a real estate development than as a unique wildlife sanctuary where school children as well as adults could peer into the wonders of creation.

As you drove away from Lehi's marsh, skirting the edge of San Leandro Bay, you came upon a sight that seemed to sum up the situation eloquently. A big snowy egret, one of the largest flying birds on earth, was standing in a marsh pool which his ancestors had probably frequented for a thousand years. But he seemed to be staring quizzically at something new: a pile of garbage and debris ten feet high. That edge of San Leandro Bay had become the Alameda city dump.

Not long after your visit to the Bay Farm Island marsh, the dredges and earth-moving machines appeared on the site. Within a few months the marsh was turned into dry land, ready for the asphalt and tract houses.

3/ WHO OWNS THE BAY?

During the early 1960's, when it became apparent that vast areas of the Bay were disappearing, many residents of the region were surprised to learn that a large part of the Bay was private property, and could be bought, sold, filled, or drained at the owner's pleasure.

About 50% of the Bay floor is owned by the state; 5% is in Federal ownership; and 23% has been granted by the state to cities and counties, most of which have had their own plans for filling. But most of the 22% that is privately owned is in the most critical part of the Bay, the shallow shoreline waters off the areas of greatest population.

The Bay began to pass from public to private ownership as soon as Americans took over California from the Mexicans — or possibly even a little sooner. Even before the treaty was signed in 1848, California's military man-on-the-spot, Brigadier General Stephen W. Kearny, granted water lots in Yerba Buena Cove to the town of San Francisco and directed that they be auctioned off to the highest bidders. The delighted owners proceeded to build wharves on their lots or to haul rock and soil from nearby Telegraph Hill and turn the water into dry ground.

When the Gold Rush brought pandemonium to San Francisco, the value of the new waterfront lots skyrocketed.

Members of the Legislature, looking for easy ways to enrich the state treasury, thought it would be a fine idea to sell some more of the Bay. They drew up a new waterfront line offshore and gave San Francisco the Bay bottom inside the line on the condition that the city would kick back to the state 24% of the revenue from sale of the "land."

The old waterfront owners, the original fillers of the Bay, were left high and dry as the new owners dumped dirt along the shore to create a newer waterfront. But they, too, were stranded two years later when the Legislature decided once again to raise funds by the simple expedient of establishing another "permanent" waterfront line and selling the water lots out to that line.

So little by little Yerba Buena Cove disappeared. And if the process by which the politicians blithely disposed of the public lands seems questionable today, it was in full accord with the ethics and outlook of the times.

This was the beginning of the era of the "Great Giveaway," which reached a climax in the decades after the Civil War when politicans in state and the national capitols freely handed over public lands, forests, and waterways to private interests without regard for public rights or needs. As Stewart L. Udall points out in *The Quiet Crisis,* ". . . Between 1850 and 1871 an area larger than France, England, Scotland and Wales was granted the railroad companies," and valuable timberlands were disposed of at prices as low as ten cents an acre. The word "conservation" was not in common use, and it had scarcely occurred to anyone that natural resources should be conserved in the long-term public interest rather than exploited for short-term private profit.

The disposal of San Francisco Bay that began with the

The Bay once covered this "reclaimed" land.

filling of Yerba Buena Cove continued under various auspices for a century thereafter. Thousands of acres were granted to cities to be leased out, and thousands more were disposed of to private owners as "tidelands" (between high and low tides), although sometimes conniving officials stretched the definition of tidelands to include vast areas of Bay bottom to depths of 18 feet, a piece of skullduggery that throws into question even some present-day titles to the underwater lands. Part of the jiggery-pokery that took place was the practice by speculators of buying up underwater "tide" lots immediately off the shoreline and then charging fantastic prices to waterfront owners for access to the Bay. Efforts to amend the laws to bring some order to the situation were only partially successful as ingenious promoters continued to find loopholes.

39

Contrasts in Waterfront living: Sausalito (left) and Tiburon

In recent decades, although the original practice of selling pieces of the Bay to private owners has been largely discontinued, similar purposes are accomplished by conditional grants from the state to cities and counties. Originally, these grants, most of which extended into the Bay beyond the privately-owned property, were mainly for purposes of harbor improvements, but in recent years the stated purposes have been broadened to include airports and various kinds of commercial and industrial uses.

Plans for the filling of these lands have been hastened by the practice of the Legislature to require as a condition of the grant that "improvements" be made within a ten-year period. In order to acquire the offshore waters, in other words, the cities have had to promise to fill them up.

The kind of chaos that has resulted from the fragmentation of ownership of the Bay has been well described by Mel Scott in *The Future of San Francisco Bay:* "One city wants to discharge a greater volume of partially treated sewage effluent into the Bay, whereas the neighboring city hopes to develop a bathing beach nearby. A land syndicate proposes to create a marina-type residential community in a shallow cove that is particularly attractive to sports fishermen. An industrial realtor plans to reclaim tidelands on which to construct factories that residents of the nearby hills will consider blights on the landscape. The clash of desires raises the question: What is in the public interest? What is best for the majority of Bay Area residents? And by what process can the public interest be determined?"

For answers to these questions, it is necessary to consider all present and possible uses of the Bay. What value does the Bay possess and what will be lost if it continues to disappear?

41

ONE of the most rewarding sights to be seen over the Bay is the visit of a flock of great white pelicans from their homes on the lakes of the Great Basin, east of the Sierra. Unlike the resident brown pelicans, they visit the Bay seasonally, usually in the spring or fall. They are among the largest flying birds on earth, with a wingspread sometimes approaching ten feet.

A flight of seventy or eighty may appear off the Embarcadero, soaring high above the surface, scarcely moving a wing. They fly with impressive dignity, their long necks curved easily back, yellow bills resting forward, white wings glinting in the sun. Effortlessly they ride the air currents, with no apparent purpose or desire other than sheer enjoyment of the sunshine and the blue Bay, unperturbed by the traffic along the shore or the boats below them. Even an occasional low-flying plane leaves them unruffled; they magnificently ignore the noisy mechanical intruder, holding their rightful place with placid dignity.

After several minutes, suddenly and without apparent signal, they all begin to turn, some in large arcs, some in small, tightly banked circles, until the entire flock is slowly revolving like a wheel or a solar system around some in-

visible sun. For perhaps fifteen minutes the formation evolves through various sizes and shapes as individuals and groups within it create their own random pattern of curving flight.

Then, with a simultaneous singleness of purpose, the wheeling formation dissolves into a long, rolling V-shaped figure that gradually merges into a single line, and the entire group is off again, paralleling the Bay shore. Each bird follows the one ahead in graceful rises and dips and swayings from side to side, like beads on a long, undulating string. An individual may vary from the formation in his own fashion, yet all unite in a marvelously harmonious whole, like a ballet whose members follow the rhythmic pattern but are free to improvise within its framework as they choose.

When the formation changes, however, the entire flock moves apparently at the same instant, as if governed by radio signals. Like many birds, the pelican possesses a cerebellum — the part of the brain governing coordination — that is in some ways more highly developed than that of the human being. What communications, imperceptible to humans, pass among them, guiding their maneuvers, is a mystery as yet unpenetrated by science.

From the most primitive mollusks in the ooze of the Bay bottom to these majestic dwellers of the sky, the life of the Bay is a single, unfolding drama of creation, a galaxy of societies as varied and complex as the cities on the shores.
— San Francisco Bay

Birds of the Bay:
nest of the pied-billed grebe; young gull; brown pelicans; American egret in flight.

Birds of the Bay: An egret in a threatened marsh, Mill Valley;
shorebirds waiting for the ebb in San Pablo Bay;
water birds over a herring run off Sausalito

4 / ON THE PACIFIC FLYWAY

"WHICH are more important, people or birds?" The questioner was arguing for conversion of a Bay wildlife marsh into a subdivision. The implication was, of course, that it was necessary to make a choice: Since there was a need for more housing to accommodate the burgeoning population, the birds would have to go.

The answer to the question is that birds are important to people, a proposition that is sanctioned by law and treaty. A treaty signed with Great Britain in 1916 to protect migratory birds stated: ". . . Many of these species . . . of great value as a source of food or in destroying insects which are injurious to forests and forage plants on the public domain, as well as to agricultural crops, both in the United States and Canada . . . are nevertheless in danger of extermination through lack of adequate protection during the nesting season or while on their way to and from their breeding grounds. . . ."

For these reasons, among others, state and federal governments have spent millions of dollars to maintain refuges and watering grounds for migratory birds. On the Pacific Flyway, one of the four principal continental routes along which the flocks move south in the fall and north in the

Modes of Bay travel: egret and Richardson Bay Bridge, Marin

spring, San Francisco Bay is the most important single stopping place. Eliminate the shallows of the Bay and you eliminate a prime habitat of most of the birds on the Pacific Flyway. Do away with the birds and you destroy natural museums of incalculable educational, recreational, and esthetic value; you also risk upsetting the balance of nature that keeps the insect populations in check — with what ominous results for the human race we can only conjecture.

Anyone with a good eye can spot four main kinds of

migratory birds along the edges of the Bay: waterfowl, including several varieties of ducks and geese and such glamorous species as the whistling swans; the shorebirds that swarm over the sand flats at low tide — avocets, willets, sandpipers, and sanderlings; gulls; and marshbirds — rails, coots, the huge blue herons, and the magnificent big white egrets.

The U. S. Bureau of Sport Fisheries and Wildlife estimates that about one million waterfowl, mostly ducks, winter on the Bay. Nearly three quarters of all the diving ducks in California come to the Bay. Two-thirds of all the canvasbacks and scaups in the state inhabit these waters and shores. Along the tidal flats and marshes there may be at times as many as 20,000 shorebirds per mile. Most of the waterfowl and shorebirds feed on the organisms that breed in the same shallow water areas that are being filled with garbage and subdivisions.

The Bay is a mecca for duck hunters. There are about 300 duck clubs in the area, and this is one of the few remaining spots in California open to all hunters free of charge.

Already thousands of acres of Bay wildlife habitat have been destroyed, increasing the importance of the remaining areas. It is not surprising that the Bureau of Sport Fisheries and Wildlife, charged with safeguarding bird populations, is opposed to further filling. "Reclamation activities should cease," the Bureau reports, "until a coordinated program for the use of all lands in the Bay Area is developed. . . . Key habitat areas of important fish and wildlife value must be safeguarded for future generations. Studies of fish and wildlife resources are needed now to establish the relationship of intertidal areas to the productivity of the entire Bay Area."

54

5 / WEALTH FROM THE WATERS

THE threatened disappearance of large parts of the Bay is a matter of direct concern not only to the birds, bird watchers and duck hunters but to the thousands of people who depend on it for their livelihood. Shipping presumably would not be put out of business by filling since the deep water channels would be kept open in any event, but other kinds of business would be eliminated or seriously curtailed by continued filling.

A large proportion of the salt used in the West comes directly out of the Bay at the rate of a million tons annually. There are 46,000 acres of salt ponds around the shallow shores producing 10 million dollars worth of salt a year. Directly dependent on this salt are scores of industries around the Bay and beyond. A multimillion-dollar cement industry depends on ancient deposits of shell on the Bay bottom. Also directly related to the Bay is a 32 million-dollar sport fishing industry and a 7 million-dollar annual trade with duck hunters. The Bay's prize sport fish, the striped bass, accounts for well over two million man-days of fishing a year. The fishermen spend money for boats, bait and fishing gear. Although much of this catch is in deep water, either within the Bay itself or in the ocean outside the heads, the fish depend on the Bay's shallows for feeding, spawning, and nursery grounds; and the organisms on which the fish feed, even in deep water, must live in the shallows for part of their life cycle. Directly dependent on the disappearing shallow areas are not only the stripers but American shad, Pacific herring, starry flounder, Pacific sand dab, smelt, anchovies, salmon, lingcod, rockfish and surf perch.

Another 30-billion dollars or more are spent every year by the owners of pleasure boats around the Bay — for the boats themselves and for supplies, maintenance, fuel storage, and docking facilities. As the Bay shrinks, opportunities for boating decrease proportionally.

These figures on the economic use of the Bay as a natural resource are miniscule compared to the Bay' economic potential if fully developed. Boat ownership, for example, increased from about 22,000 boats in 1950 to 45,000 in 1960 to about 75,000 in 1965. If new docks and shoreline parks are created the figure doubtless will soar as the population increases. Hunting and fishing expenditures will also rise swiftly — if filling and pollution do not continue to destroy fish and wildlife habitats.

Perhaps the most fascinating prospect is the possibility that the Bay can become a vitally important food source for the future. According to U. S. Department of Commerce Studies in 1960, the Bay Area population was expected to double within 25 years and quadruple within 50. Despite the consequent quadrupled need for food, urban expansion continues to pave over Californias valuable agricultural land at the rate of 140,000 acres every year.

Dr. Francis P. Felice, Professor of Biology at the University of San Francisco, states: "The rapid growth of the world's population has set biologists to exploring every

A vitally important food source

possible avenue in the attempt to keep food production sufficient for the number of people the world will soon have to support. One of the most important areas being explored for food potential is our marine waters, which cover 72% of the surface of this planet.''

The water areas, Dr. Felice indicates, could produce several times as much food as equivalent land areas. But there are difficulties to ''farming'' the open sea, he explains, and the most promising possibilities lie in inland waters. ''The perfect example of this is San Francisco Bay, which is warm, shallow, and has sufficient sun and minerals for optimum plant growth.'' Potentially, Dr. Felice indicates, the Bay could produce ten times as much food value per acre as an equivalent land area. ''If San Francisco Bay were filled completely and planted with corn, under the best conditions enough feed would be produced for 60 million pounds of beef a year. If, however, the Bay were left alone and the algae farmed, sufficient feed could be produced to yield 600 million pounds of beef a year. . . .''

Algae are a group of plants that grow in water, includ- ing varieties commonly known as seaweed. Some kinds are also used as food for humans. ''Algal soup'' is a common Japanese dish. Raising algae crops in the Bay would not interfere with the use of the same areas for recreation or for greatly expanded fisheries — an efficient kind of aquatic multiple use.

Continued chaotic filling of the critical shallow edges of the Bay, Dr. Felice notes, is ''likely to destroy unknowingly the very parts of the Bay that are productive. If, for ex- ample, you were to eliminate the Bay floor down to the three- fathom mark tomorrow, almost certainly you would turn the remainder into a biological desert.''

San Francisco Bay, then, is a natural resource in more than a figurative sense. It is a source of economic value as surely as are forests, soil, and minerals in the earth. Its pro- ductive potential has barely been tapped. To destroy the Bay is to destroy a source of wealth for future generations.

6 / TEN THOUSAND TONS A DAY

TOSSING the contents of the slop pail out the living room window is a practice not generally looked upon with favor these days, but that is almost exactly what local communities are doing when they heave their accumulated refuse into San Francisco Bay.

As a result, many parts of the Bay have been converted into a series of monumental garbage dumps. The most familiar, and obnoxious, of these dumps is the infamous "Candlestink Cove" area along the principal highway approach to San Francisco. Here, some years ago, near the city of Brisbane the freeway was extended across the mouth of the cove for two miles. The several hundred acres of water inshore, which might have become a prime water-recreation center, were preempted by the refuse interests and turned into a fuming sump alongside the highway.

By 1965 the filled-in cove was mercifully screened by vegetation; the aromas of refuse assaulted the nostrils of motorists less frequently than before; and motorists approaching the city could still look eastward at a superb view of the Bay and its far shores. This was the last remaining place along the so-called Bayshore freeway where the Bay was still visible. In that same year, however, the dump was

being extended across the road. The main highway entrance to San Francisco was about to be flanked by stinking garbage dumps on both sides when residents of Brisbane, resentful that their offshore waters had become San Francisco's refuse dump, revolted and voted to cancel contracts their own city officials had signed with the garbage firms. Eventually a compromise was reached, permitting completion of the filling of certain diked areas on the Bay side of the freeway but leaving most of the shoreline in open water.

There are 31 other refuse disposal sites around the shores of the Bay, "sanitary land fills" where dirt is spread over the refuse to cover it up — theoretically. The dirt has to be hauled from hills by trucks roaring through business and residential areas, creating traffic hazards, dust, and general uproar — not to mention the scarring of the hills themselves.

Water pollution officials frequently warn the garbage dumpers about fouling the waters by inadequate coverage.

60

The cities of San Mateo county have been the worst offenders. Daly City, on the ocean side of the Peninsula, has dumped "sanitary fill" refuse along the tops of sea cliffs, where it has spilled down to shore areas below. There the waves continually undermine the mountain of garbage and transport it along the shore, strewing litter even on San Francisco's beaches miles away.

It is incredible that this medieval behavior is still tolerated in American society. It is not only tolerated, it is seldom questioned. In response to complaints, officials usually fall back on the standard answer: "We have to dump it someplace."

Admittedly the problem is staggering. At the rate of four-and-a-half pounds per person per day, the city of San Francisco produces nearly 1800 tons of garbage every day of the year. The entire Bay Area, with a population of some four million, yields up about 10,000 tons each day. With expected population growth, the continued accumulation would be enough, within the lifetimes of most people now living, to bury the city of San Francisco six feet deep in garbage.

It is quite possible to handle garbage in civilized ways. Incineration, the method in use in many cities, has been eliminated in the Bay Area because of the smog problem. New techniques may minimize air pollution, but incineration still leaves residues and unburnables amounting to as much as half of the original volume. It also wastes valuable organic materials. The same may be said for most schemes to dump garbage into the ocean, even if there were a fool-proof method of insuring that the garbage would not return to litter the shores. Dumping it in remote areas is equally wasteful; the notion that unprocessed urban refuse can "fertilize" the desert is nonsense.

In a time of exploding population and depleted resources, we can no longer afford to waste immense quantities of reclaimable material. Refuse should be regarded as a resource to be conserved for use. Organic wastes came from the earth and should be returned to the earth to enrich the soil.

Richard A. Peters, of the California Department of Public Health, points out that there are at least two methods of reclaiming garbage. Both require separation of organic from inorganic refuse, which can be done either by the householder or by the processor. Metals and other inorganic material can be reclaimed for use in manufacturing.

"One method of handling organic garbage is destructive distillation," Peters reports. "It involves converting the refuse to carbon products, such as charcoal briquettes, with such side products as chemicals, coal tar, therapeutic drugs, and methane gas, which can be used to dilute natural gas.

"Another method is to convert the organic refuse into

aerobic compost, which is good humus-like material and can be combined with other elements to make a complete soil additive. The product is a clean, odorless substance that does not attract insects or rodents. It can be baled and occupies one-fourth to one-third the space required for unprocessed refuse.''

The initial cost of composting may be as much as twice the present cost of dumping the garbage in the Bay, but Peters believes that most or all of the difference could be made up by selling the material to farmers and gardeners and by using it elsewhere for conservation purposes. For example, it can be moistened, impregnated with seeds, and sprayed on bare soil for reforestation or replanting areas burned over, logged over, or denuded by highway cuts.

The biggest obstacle to this method is a temporary one — the development of markets for the compost as a soil additive. Even if it were not initially possible for a city or region to sell its compost material on a commercial basis, it would be socially advantageous to distribute it below cost in order to preserve for higher uses the areas where the garbage might be dumped — whether the Bay or the canyons and ravines used by some communities for disposal.

The technicians have done their job in developing disposal processes. It is now up to the economists and public officials to do theirs. It is time our garbage disposal methods were brought into the 20th century.

Meantime, there is enough room in existing dumps to take all Bay Area refuse until about 1980 with no further bay filling except in areas already diked off for dumps. The problem of distributing the refuse is primarily political and can only be solved on a regional basis.

7/ THE ESSENTIAL SHOALS

SINCE cities first learned to deal with their liquid waste by pumping it away, they have customarily collected the sewage for disposal into nearby rivers, lakes, and bays. San Francisco Bay is no exception.

Immediately before and during World War II, the volume of sewage going into the Bay had reached such proportions that fish were killed and the stench of the pollution spread for many miles beyond the shores. University of California students during those years, whiffing the aromas drifting across the campus, five miles from the Bay, dubbed the fragrance the "East Bay Stink."

The situation became such a menace to health that the State Department of Public Health and the San Francisco Bay Regional Water Quality Control Board, created in 1949, insisted that local governments build sewage treatment plants. As a result the water quality has improved; fish are more abundant; and the "East Bay Stink" has almost entirely disappeared. Yet the sewage problem is still serious.

Increases in population, industry, and home garbage-disposal units have resulted in large volumes of sewage, requiring continual expansion of facilities. Local officials are reluctant to spend money for this purpose and have to be prodded continually by the Water Quality Control Boards to do so. The consequent lag keeps the Bay dirty.

A further source of trouble is the Sacramento River, and other tributary waters; the board has no control over pollution from upstream. And raw sewage is still dumped freely into the Bay from ships and small boats. The city of San Francisco is possibly the worst offender. Its sewers are combined with storm drains. During heavy rains, the runoff overloads the treatment plants, and raw sewage of every description litters the beaches of the Golden Gate.

Another pollution problem is that filling of the shallow areas further reduces the Bay's capacity to handle the sewage that is dumped into it, processed or otherwise. Because of stronger sunlight, a large expanse of shallow water oxidizes sewage much more quickly than does the same volume of deep water. Developers often claim that even if all the shoreline waters were filled there would still be plenty of Bay left. The argument is spurious. These shoals are essential to the Bay's chain of life, and their necessity for health and sanitation constitutes an additional reason for their preservation. Eliminate the shallows and the Bay would become a stinking cesspool.

Still another problem is the plan to dump waste agricultural waters from the San Joaquin Valley into the Bay through the San Luis Drain. These runoff waters, high in salts, fertilizers, and the residue of pesticides sprayed on crops, would be transported down the west side of the valley and poured into the Bay at Antioch.

The Federal Water Pollution Control Administration has concluded that this proposed drain would be harmful to the Bay and has recommended that no discharge from the drain be permitted until 1972. Meantime sewage treatment

Sewage transport: ebbing waters of the Bay outside the Gate

plants could be constructed and tested. A further proposal would be a single giant interceptor sewage system that would collect the treated flow of the San Luis Drain as well as that of all areas around the Bay's shores and carry it to the oceans, bypassing the Bay. Unfortunately there have been no studies of the cumulative effects on the ocean or the shoreline waters if they were required to receive the sewage of major urban areas in California.

In the long run, in this region of water shortages, it would seem that the only prudent way to dispose of sewage would be to reclaim it for use. It has long been evident that sewage can be "purified" into fresh drinking water and the residues used for soil enrichment. Like solid waste, liquid sewage is a potential resource to be recycled back into the economy. With the growing threat that the human population will outrun available resources, it is no longer feasible to waste any element that may be vital to human survival.

In any case it is possible to build sewage facilities that would make all parts of the Bay safe for swimming and other water contact sports. The cost would doubtless be high. But the issue is whether this Bay is to continue to be used as a convenient sewer or whether it has higher uses for which residents should be willing to pay a price.

8/THE SUMMER BREEZE

THE continuing destruction of San Francisco Bay by filling would have disastrous effects in many directions, but possibly the most pervasive result of all would be its impact on the Bay Area's climate.

You can pollute the waters, ruin the oyster beds and destroy the wildlife refuges; you can cut off the life chain of the striped bass and other highly prized fish; you can fill shoreline areas needed for water parks and yacht harbors; you can silt up small boat marinas and landlock shoreline residences; but the people directly affected are only a handful compared to the millions involved when you tamper with the climate.

There is no doubt that even minor fills change in some degree the weather of the immediately adjacent areas. Every body of water larger than a puddle has some effect on the climate of the land around its edges. Householders on Lake Merritt in Oakland, for example, have slightly cooler summers and slightly warmer winters than areas a few blocks away. On a much larger scale the Great Lakes cool their shores in summer and warm them in the winter. Because of the cooling influence of Lake Michigan, for example, most of Michigan has cooler summers than comparable non-lake states.

The greatest influences on climate are, of course, the oceans. Without the Pacific to temper its weather, California would suffer the searing heat and numbing cold of Nevada and Utah and Colorado.

On another scale, the same phenomenon takes place around the shores of San Francisco Bay. The Bay Area would be as hot as the Central Valley in the summer if it were not for two moderating influences: the ocean breeze blowing through the Golden Gate (and to a lesser extent through the other gaps in the Coast Range) and the Bay itself. Without the Bay, the marine winds through the Gate would soon be heated by their passage over the land and would have far less cooling effect. But the air-conditioning function of the Bay is not limited to keeping down the temperature of the ocean breezes. Even when there is no movement of air from the ocean the Bay generates its own winds.

Because air masses tend to move from a cooler to a warmer area, the air over the Bay on a summer day, cooled by contact with the water, moves toward the sun-heated shores, creating an onshore breeze. In the afternoon when land temperatures are highest, the breeze increases, dying down again at evening when land and water temperatures become more nearly equal.

This writer can remember on a summer afternoon leaving Huddart Park, in the hills behind Woodside, where we were plagued by heat and yellow jackets, and retreating a few miles to Flood Park near the Bay shore, where a pleasant breeze was blowing off the water, too cool for yellow jackets but very refreshing for humans. The temperature back in the hills was near 90, but on the Bay shore, cooled by air blowing off water in the 60s, the mercury was brought down into the comfortable 70s.

*The air as a sewer: smog south of Berkeley;
polluters at San Francisco Airport*

Filling the shallow areas off Menlo Park and Palo Alto, for example, would eliminate the water-cooled breezes and give those cities a summer climate more comparable to that of San Jose. Even San Jose would have hotter summers if some Bay breezes did not reach there. Diminish the Bay and you give such shoreline cities as San Mateo and Redwood City and San Rafael summer weather closer to that of Gilroy or Livermore or Tracy.

Less familiar than the air-conditioning effect of the Bay in summer is its warming effect in winter. The water stays relatively warm — in the 50s or high 40s — while the land temperatures during cold spells drop into the 30s at night, and sometimes lower. In bayshore communities early morning winter temperatures, buoyed by the relative warmth of the Bay, seldom drop below freezing, but ice will form in the hill areas farther from the water. Even in a cold snap Palo Alto rarely goes below 32 degrees, yet temperatures in the 20s are often recorded by the weather station at Searsville, a few miles inland.

Similarly San Rafael in winter is warmer than Fairfax, a short distance inland. Both communities would be colder if substantial portions of the Bay were eliminated. Since freezing will kill a good many kinds of plants, a few degrees of temperature may be a matter of botanical life or death.

Thus the Bay acts as a giant thermostat, not only cooling the land in summer but heating it in winter, moderating the climate not only of its immediate shores but of the entire basin around it.

The most threatening climatic byproduct of destruction of the Bay would be increased smog. Whenever the prevailing winds die down, a miasma of smog begins to rise in the mornings from chimneys and car exhausts, begriming the

Tides in the sky: winter fog from Marin

air. The atmosphere around the Bay, normally bright and burnished and crystal clear, begins to turn to a bilious gray-brown, tinged with mustard-gas yellow. The far shores become invisible. But in the afternoons, when the sun heats land temperatures sufficiently, the Bay as air conditioner goes into action and much of the smog is dissipated by the onshore breezes. This effect is particularly pronounced during the early fall and late spring smog seasons.

To the degree that the Bay is filled, air circulation will diminish and smog will increase. Not one of the developers dumping dirt into the Bay and replacing open water with subdivisions or freeways or garbage or factory sites believes that his fill could possibly affect the climate of the entire region. But in the aggregate that is exactly what fills would do.

9 / THE COMING EARTHQUAKE

LURKING silently in the background of all discussions about the filling of the Bay is the ominous question of earthquake risk. Toward future earthquakes in general, Californians have always maintained an ostrich posture, preferring to close their eyes and ears entirely rather than face the facts and take measures to minimize damage.

This attitude has carried over to the earthquake dangers involved in Bay filling. Although many geologists are convinced that building on Bay mud in this earthquake zone may be a risky business, they are usually cautiously objective and reluctant to engage in public controversy. On the occasions when geologists have spoken out, they have been met with storms of protest from the filler-developers, who hire expert consultants to tell them and the public that there is no danger.

Without going into all the detailed charges and counter-charges, it is possible to separate fact from opinion.

It is a fact that earthquake shaking on Bay mud (or other watersoaked soil) is greater in magnitude than on any other kind of ground. In its seismic reactions, Bay mud is about as stable as tomato aspic; the ground motion of an earthquake is amplified many times. How great the jolt may be depends on several variables, including the type of soil, the kind of fill laid upon it, the shape of the bedrock bottom beneath the mud, and the mud's depth. It is notable that the greatest recorded depth of mud and other unconsolidated sediments anywhere in the Bay Area is at Bay Farm Island, where the city of Alameda approved of plans for a subdivision without inquiring into the matter of earthquake risk. Bedrock, according to the U. S. Geological Survey maps, lies several hundred feet below the surface and at one point is only reached at a depth of 1000 feet.

It is a fact that the greatest earthquake damage in San Francisco in 1906 took place on Bay fill, including a large part of downtown San Francisco. Much has been learned since about how to fill and how to build for earthquake safety, but even in recent quakes the damage on soft, water-soaked soil has been greater than elsewhere.

It is a fact that geologists expect another earthquake in this region as strong or stronger than the quake of 1906, although they cannot predict when it will come.

It is a fact that it is demonstrably possible to construct buildings that will stand up well against shakes even as violent as those to be expected on Bay mud. The Ferry Building, for example, constructed on Bay mud, was not seriously damaged in 1906. Some well-built structures, even high-rise buildings, have survived, with little damage, quakes such as those in Mexico City in 1957 and in Anchorage, Alaska, in 1964, but other modern buildings in both quakes were badly damaged or collapsed. In Anchorage, for example, one brand-new concrete lift-slab building flattened in a heap; after the shake its six floors all lay on the ground like a stack of pancakes. The greatest damage in both the Mexico City and Anchorage quakes was on soft, unconsolidated soils similar to some soils beneath the Bay. Owing to the whip-lash effect, tall buildings on such soils are particularly risky.

The critical question is whether the buildings on the shaky ground are actually constructed with the necessary extra safety factor. In many cases they are not. The serious-ly cracked-up or collapsed major buildings in Anchorage in 1964 were all found to have structural defects. With com-petitive pressures to keep costs down, some builders, on Bay fill and elsewhere, are under strong temptation to cut corners and avoid incurring extra expense.

Complicating the whole picture is the fact that what con-stitutes an adequate safety factor may be a matter of opin-ion. No one, in order to save money, is going to design a building he thinks is unsafe. But his opinion of what is un-safe may be influenced by his need to minimize costs. The Anchorage quake ruined many buildings that were all be-lieved to be safe by their designers and builders — evidence that architects, contractors and soil engineers are not in-fallible. Neither are city building inspectors, who are not likely themselves to be qualified structural engineers or ge-ologists or soil engineers. Moreover, enforcement of building codes, which themselves may or may not be adequate, is often a haphazard process, and there is little to prevent a builder from taking short cuts when the inspector is not looking, which is most of the time. In any case, building codes do not require special earthquake design for buildings on weak soil.

All this uncertainty accounts for the fact that insurance companies normally charge an extra 25 per cent to insure buildings on filled ground. Of course, in some areas the risk may be less, in other areas considerably above 25 per cent.

In addition to the direct damage from earthquake shaking, there are other possible causes of trouble on filled ground. Even though the Bay mud is covered with "engineered fill" — scientifically selected rock and soil that itself may be solid — some authorities believe that the fill may still be loosened by the motion of soft mud beneath it.

In this view, a quake might shake down the unconsolidated, water-soaked mud so that it settles unevenly. Places where the mud beneath the fill is deep, for example, may settle more than places where it is shallow. Or the bedrock beneath the mud may be steep and slippery, and the mud might slide down the incline when jostled by an earthquake. Conceivably the ground beneath a single building can settle unevenly, tipping it up. In Niigata, Japan, in 1964, a quake knocked a multi-story building into a horizontal position, although it was structurally undamaged otherwise. A further hazard on built-up marshlands may be the danger of flooding from earthquake-breached dikes.

The possibility of these kinds of damage is largely a matter of opinion. Some people, including those engaged in filling, claim that with adequate precaution the risk is so slight as to be disregarded. They may be supported by consulting soil engineers. Yet some geologists are convinced that the risk is great enough to justify prohibition of all further building on fills. Still other experts believe that not enough is known about these matters either way and that the first priority is research.

It should be pointed out that the extra earthquake risk of building on Bay mud may be comparable to high risks in building on precipitous hillsides or fault zones. Unfortunately, these are all common practices in the Bay Area.

Even without significant earthquakes, there has already

been some damage to hillside buildings from landslides and to filled areas from settling. At points on the Bayshore freeway south of San Francisco, the road has a slight rollercoaster effect where the settling of fill has been uneven. At a San Rafael school built on Bay fill, the yard has sunk away from the building. The Bay Bridge Toll Plaza area is continually sinking, and westbound cars leaving the toll station go down a slight ramp that has to be repaired frequently as the fill subsides. One building in the area tilts about a foot out of line. All this, of course, is only a very minor token of what could happen in a big seismic shakedown.

A large proportion of the damage in Anchorage in 1964, particularly to residences, was caused by landslides. But this kind of landslide does not necessarily require steep slopes. It may take place as a slumping action on gentle slopes.

It is scarcely an adequate safeguard to leave judgment about earthquake safety on fills to the people who profit from filling. In all areas of high earthquake risk, the burden of proof should be on the developer to show that he is taking whatever extra measures may be necessary. His evidence should be submitted to an impartial board of structural engineers, geologists and soil engineers who can represent the public and are in no way interested in the construction projects, financially or otherwise.

At the very least the public should be fully informed as to the risks involved. This is an urgent matter of public safety; irresponsible Bay filling in the future could lead to a disaster of the magnitude of Anchorage or greater.

10 / THE POLITICS OF FILL

ALTHOUGH the plans of the San Francisco Bay fillers, both public and private, have continually expanded with rising population and prosperity, it may be enlightening to examine the status of fill plans around the Bay as of mid-1965. This was just before the creation of the San Francisco Bay Conservation and Development Commission, established to regulate Bay fill projects until a regional master plan could be developed.

It is noteworthy that without exception the planned fills were in the Bay's critical zones, the shoreline areas that are the principal nurseries for fish and their food, and the main feeding grounds for millions of waterfowl — the same areas that provide close-in views of water for the bayside communities, that moderate the weather of the immediate shores, that offer the best opportunities for shoreline and water recreation.

Consider, for example, San Mateo County — the peninsula below San Francisco. In the late 1950's the county drew a master plan for future land use. In many respects the plan was a good one, balancing residential and commercial development with large areas to be reserved for recreation and open space, particularly on the county's oceanward slope. But along the Bay side of the peninsula, the planners decided to allow filling of the shallow shoreline waters, reserving a few areas for parks and marinas.

The state legislature had decreed that there should eventually be another freeway parallel to the present Bayshore freeway, but had not designated a location. The San Mateo planners chose a location two to three miles out in the water so that the new "Bayfront" freeway would skirt the outer edge of the San Francisco Airport and leave plenty of room, along the rest of the shoreline, for "development" or filling of the area between the two freeways. The Bay and shoreline area involved would amount to some 23 square miles — a region about half the size of San Francisco.

Where would all the dirt come from for such a vast fill? Luckily a convenient source was handy — the San Bruno Mountains, a high ridge flanked by green rolling hills at the northern end of the county, providing a monumental entrance to San Francisco from the south. Engineers reported that something like a billion cubic yards of dirt and rock could be gouged from the mountains and dumped into the Bay. It made little difference, apparently, that the hills constituted a prime natural recreation area and has been so designated on the master plan.

By mid-1965 several major fills were under way or projected in the inter-freeway area outlined by the San Mateo County plan, notably at South San Francisco, San Francisco Airport, Burlingame, Redwood City, and Menlo Park. The Redwood Shores residential project, an extension of Redwood City, was being planned for a 4500-acre area of former marshland that had long ago been diked for salt ponds. Most of this area had been designated in the county master plan as recreational land and open space. In Burlingame a big fill for industrial and commercial use was occupying a large plot the master plan had reserved as a water area. Such breaches of a master plan made it obvious that municipalities and commercial interests could invoke a master plan where it suited their convenience and ignore it elsewhere.

San Mateo County offered a typical example of the politics of Bay fill. Back in the wooded foothills of the Santa Cruz Mountains, developers were bulldozing and scraping away hillsides at a tremendous rate for the new subdivisions and high-rise apartments. Normally they would have had to pay somebody to haul away the prodigious amounts of dirt and rock excavated, but here they instead were able to sell it to truckers who hauled it down to the water's edge and resold it for Bay fill. Add to these enterprises the banks and loan companies backing the projects and there is a formidable phalanx of commercial interests all profiting handsomely from the filling operation and all in a position to put pressure on local agencies to keep the dirt moving from the mountains to the Bay, despite the complaints of local residents about the noise, dust, and traffic hazards created by the convoys of trucks. Here, surely, was eloquent rebuttal to those who claimed that the fate of the Bay should remain in the hands of local agencies.

San Mateo County was not alone in its ambitious Bay fill plans. In mid-1965, Bay Bridge users were jolted by the news that the Port of Oakland was applying for a permit that would enable it to fill a two-square-mile area of the Bay from the toll plaza almost to Treasure Island, obliterating the view of open water from the bridge approach.

San Francisco had a plan almost equally ambitious. Bay-side Candlestick Park, where baseball fans could arrive by boat, was slated to be left high and dry by a fill for industrial purposes extending about a mile offshore.

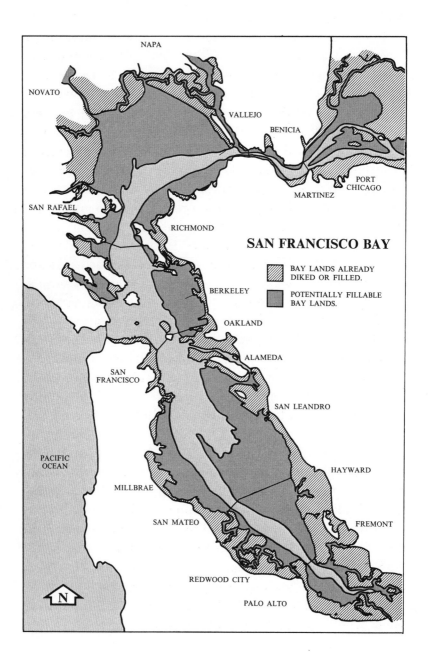

NAPA

NOVATO

VALLEJO

BENICIA

PORT
CHICAGO

MARTINEZ

SAN RAFAEL

RICHMOND

SAN FRANCISCO BAY

BAY LANDS ALREADY
DIKED OR FILLED.

POTENTIALLY FILLABLE
BAY LANDS.

BERKELEY

OAKLAND

ALAMEDA

SAN
FRANCISCO

SAN LEANDRO

PACIFIC
OCEAN

HAYWARD

MILLBRAE

SAN MATEO

FREMONT

REDWOOD CITY

PALO ALTO

N

Another Port of Oakland proposal was fill for an extension of Oakland Airport covering five square miles of the Bay. Immediately southwest of the airport the Trojan Powder Company intended to fill about 1,400 acres, a scheme that conflicted with plans of the city of San Leandro to acquire and develop the water area within its own city limits primarily for recreation.

Still another Port of Oakland fill, also for industrial purposes, was gradually turning most of San Leandro Bay into dry land. This area has long been a state game refuge, protecting the wildfowl from hunters but not from fillers.

Immediately west, the city of Alameda had given the green light to the developer planning to fill the northwest tidelands of Bay Farm Island. Bird authorities feared that if tideland habitats continue to be destroyed, the birds would increasingly retreat to the vicinity of the Oakland Airport, threatening the safety of jet aircraft.

Emeryville was extending itself farther into the Bay, and the Santa Fe railroad had an elaborate scheme to develop vast water areas it owned off Emeryville, Berkeley, El Cerrito, Albany and Richmond. After an unfriendly reception the Santa Fe plan was withdrawn, at least temporarily.

The city of Richmond, which had 33 miles of shoreline but only 65 feet of publicly owned access to the Bay, was planning to fill most of its tidelands for industry. Already Richmond's northern embayment was partly occupied by one of the region's largest dumps, importing garbage from Marin County to supplement the local refuse. To the south, proposed fills would have extended from the mainland around 45-acre Brooks Island, a place of great natural beauty, used for biological and archeological research by college and university groups. There was talk of leveling the hilly island for fill material. (In 1968, Brooks Island was rescued by the East Bay Regional Park District, which was acquiring it for recreation. However, there was still the possibility of large-scale filling near the island for a municipal airport or other purposes.)

Across the Bay in Marin County, fill plans of San Rafael and Corte Madera were keyed to the presumed location of a new offshore freeway. San Rafael's master plan would have filled about 75 per cent of its 4300 acres of tidelands, including most of the waters around the two historic Marin Islands, last redoubt of the Indian chief from whom the county took its name and presently one of the last roosting places of American egrets, among the largest flying birds on earth. Public protest prompted a new look at the San Rafael master plan, however, and pending further study San Rafael Bay was deleted from the plan.

Neighboring Corte Madera expected to use most of its marshlands for industry, reserving a small-boat lagoon inshore from the presumed new freeway fill. Both here and off San Rafael, the Bay bottom was privately owned, and there was nothing to stop the owners from converting it to dry land.

Fortunately, the Marin Conservation League over a period of years had purchased considerable tideland acreage for preservation in a natural state. One result was the admirable Audubon Wildlife Refuge in Richardson Bay, the region's finest example of private action to save an invaluable heritage. It was the kind of superb outdoor museum of natural wonders that every city and town should have. Yet it represented an opportunity that would be denied to other communities without an enforceable master plan for the entire Bay.

Offhand, the remedy for the ongoing destruction of the Bay seemed simple: outlaw filling. But the picture was too complex for such easy answers. Consider, for example, the plight of Sausalito. There are few more picturesque communities anywhere — including the shores of the Mediterranean — than the town that climbs the wooded hillside north of the Golden Gate and looks out over the surface of the Bay to San Francisco. Yet beginning in 1964 Sausalito was faced with plans of a private corporation for a $10 million commercial development to be built on a fill protruding 1000 feet into the Bay and extending for 2000 feet, or more than seven blocks, along the waterfront.

Where there is now a shining expanse of water and a small sand bar, there would be 20 buildings, including 130 apartment units, 160 hotel rooms, two restaurants, a coffee shop, boat facilities and a shopping area. About half of the fill would be covered by parking lots.

The corporate developers insisted, with some justification, that the plans were good ones: about half of their property would be devoted to a yacht harbor, and the buildings would be tastefully designed. Small pieces of the property would be open to the public as parks.

But all this is beside the point. In a location that did not involve filling in the Bay, this might be a commendable development. But planted in the waters off-shore, it would destroy unique values of Sausalito as a bayside community. Added to similar fills that have been made or are planned along other shorelines, it would be one more violation of the Bay as open space, one more move in the Bay's piecemeal destruction.

Like most other developers eager to fill in the waters along the shores, the corporation planning the Sausalito fill

failed to consider the total impact on the Bay. It had no studies made to determine whether the fill would cause silting up of Sausalito's present yacht harbor. It took no account of the effect of the fill on the Bay's fish and wildlife, which depend on the shallow shoreline waters. It took no account of studies of the Bay's ecology being made by the

Fill for race track parking at Albany

University of California's Sanitary Engineering Research Laboratory, the California Department of Fish and Game, and the U. S. Department of the Interior.

Fearful of the threat of unregulated filling to fish and wildlife, the Federal agency recommended that "piecemeal reclamation of tidelands, marshes, and submerged lands in the Bay Area be prohibited until a coordinated land-use program for the Bay Area is completed.'' The State Fish and Game Department heartily agreed.

Sausalito, overwhelmingly opposed to the fill, took decisive action. The city council passed the region's first moratorium on Bay fill, prohibiting the proposed project, and any other filling, until the completion of a master plan for the entire Bay. The developers promptly responded by suing the city. They argued that they had purchased the underwater lots for the purpose of developing them, that they must protect their investment or suffer financial loss, and that no one could legally deprive them of the right to develop their property. The central problem is one of the oldest riddles of democracy: how to balance private rights with public rights. At stake around the shores of San Francisco Bay is the right of communities to preserve and enhance their waterfronts. To deny a community that right would be to destroy environmental values that belong not only to the present community but to future generations. It is not evident as yet how these conflicting private and public interests are to be resolved. But they will never be resolved unless the public interest is made clear and declared vigorously at every opportunity. The case of Berkeley illustrates what can be accomplished.

JUST after sundown the Bay is a pool of light in the darkening evening. It seems to have absorbed the sun's radiation during the day and to have stored it up for this time when the sky's light is dying. Against the rim of the far hills the silver-gray surface gives the illusion of being curved.

In this brief moment, when the buildings along the shores have been almost absorbed into the darkness, there comes a quick impression that the shoreline cities have vanished and the scene appears as it did before the coming of man; the only realities are the glowing Bay, the black hills, and the sky.

Then, almost imperceptibly, the lights along the far shores begin to glitter in the still clear air — the diamond constellation of Sausalito on its hillside, the scattered points of light across Belvedere and Tiburon, the dense nebulae of Richmond, Berkeley, and Oakland along the eastern foothills.

Momentarily, the Bay holds the last light of day, then disappears into blackness. Only the lamps on the bridges, swinging like strings of amber jewels over the gulf, are reflected in shimmering paths across the dark water. Else-

where, under a clear moonless sky, the Bay is an immense void, a place of absolute dark, like an abyss of infinite depth.

High on the rim of the great bowl of hills around the Bay the aircraft beacons flash their signal in rapid rhythm, which is repeated by the red warning lights on the towers of the bridges and by the lighthouses along the shore. From the mountains to the bridges to the Bay the signal is passed to the sea; and the circling sweep of the Alcatraz light is answered by quick flashes from Point Bonita, from the lightship beyond the bar, and from the great beacon on the Farallones.

— San Francisco Bay

11 / REBELLION IN BERKELEY

In 1962, Berkeley residents learned of a plan by that city to fill a large expanse of its offshore waters. Berkeley owns 4,000 acres of the Bay, roughly equal to the present land area of that city. By eliminating the water it would be able to double its size — a supreme civic achievement in this era of municipal imperialism.

The reactions of many residents to this gradual destruction of the Bay were expressed in resentment, rage, and, eventually, political action. Among Berkeleyites outraged at the prospect of losing most of the shining expanse of water offshore were Mrs. Clark Kerr, Mrs. Donald McLaughlin, and Mrs. Charles Gulick. The three university wives asked some Bay Area conservation leaders to meet at the Gulick home on Grizzly Peak Boulevard one night to see what could be done. Out of that meeting came the Save San Francisco Bay Association.

Unlike a good many well-intentioned but ineffective conservationists who feel that indignation is enough, the Save-the-Bay people did their homework: they consulted economists about the feasibility of the proposed fill; they talked to engineers, city planners, and sociologists; and they confronted the Berkeley city council with an impressive array of hard facts.

Ultimately the Bay became a top political issue in Berkeley. As a consequence the city's fill plan was abandoned, the Santa Fe plan to fill in offshore areas was temporarily withdrawn, and Berkeley planners went to work on a landscaped shoreline that would take full advantage of the Bay for recreation.

The Save-the-Bay movement spread from Berkeley around the other shores and was given further impetus by the publication of Mel Scott's well-documented attack on chaotic filling, *The Future of San Francisco Bay*.

San Francisco's State Senator "J" Eugene McAteer took up the cause and conducted a four-month series of legislative hearings on the Bay which resulted in the McAteer "Save-the-Bay" bill. Carloads of Save-the-Bay conservationists converged on Sacramento to testify whenever a hearing on the bill was announced. Astute political navigation by McAteer, and by Assemblyman Nicholas Petris in the lower house, piloted the bill past the legislative shoals with surprising success. The bill was passed by both houses in June of 1965 — a legislative triumph for the Save-the Bay movement just three years after its inception at the historic first meeting on Grizzly Peak Boulevard.

It was plain that the McAteer-Petris Act was merely a necessary first step and not a panacea. However, in the language of the act the Legislature made a significant declaration of policy and set a notable precedent, indicating that "the present uncoordinated, haphazard manner in which San Francisco Bay is being filled threatens the Bay itself and is therefore inimical to the welfare of both present and future residents of the area surrounding the Bay; that while some individual fill projects may be necessary and desirable for the needs of the entire Bay region . . . , the fact remains that no governmental mechanism exists for evaluating individual projects as to their effect on the entire Bay; and that further piecemeal filling of the Bay may place serious restrictions on navigation on the Bay, may destroy the irreplaceable feeding and breeding grounds of fish and wildlife in the Bay, may adversely affect the quality of Bay waters and even the quality of air in the area, and would therefore be harmful to the needs of the present and future population of the Bay region.''

The act established the San Francisco Bay Conservation and Development Commission (BCDC) to make ''a detailed study of all the characteristics of the Bay, including the quality, quantity, and movement of Bay waters, . . . the ecological balance of the Bay, and the economic interests in the Bay, including the needs of the Bay Area population for industry and for employment.

''. . . The study should examine all present and proposed uses of the Bay and its shoreline and . . . should lead to the preparation of a comprehensive and enforceable plan for the conservation of the water of the Bay and the development of its shoreline.'' The plan was to be submitted to the 1969 Legislature, along with recommendations for its enforcement by a permanent agency to supplant the BCDC.

While the Bay master plan was being prepared (in cooperation with the Bay Area Transportation Study and the Association of Bay Area Governments) the commission was empowered ''to issue or deny permits, after public hearings, for any proposed project that involves placing fill in the Bay or extracting submerged materials from the Bay.''

Although the act's definition of the Bay included both the shoals outside the Golden Gate (the San Francisco Bar) and the marshlands (land lying five feet above sea level), it excluded all areas of the Bay "not subject to tidal action." Diked waters such as the salt ponds, could be filled without permit from the BCDC — and doubtless would be whenever the price of land rose to the point at which it was more profitable to fill than to produce salt. Some pond areas have already reached this point, notably at Redwood Shores, the 4300-acre planned development at Redwood City, designed to house 60,000 people by 1980.

Excluded also from the McAteer-Petris Act were projects under way before the BCDC came into existence on September 17, 1965. Some last-minute scrambling cleared the way for the commencement of work on the Bay Farm Island subdivision just in time to beat the deadline. The result has been the obliteration of the principal Bay Farm Island wildlife area in the dubious name of progress.

The commission was composed of 27 members, including representatives of various governmental bodies concerned with the Bay and five public members appointed by the Governor. During the three years of the commission's existence as a temporary agency, its members were confronted with more than 50 applications for filling. The McAteer-Petris Act stated: "A permit may be granted for a project if the project is either (1) necessary to the health, safety or welfare of the public in the entire bay area, (2) of such a nature that it will not adversely affect the comprehensive plan being prepared."

The commission's able staff, headed by Executive Director Joseph E. Bodovitz, and most of the members of the commission, under Chairman Melvin B. Lane, held closely to the spirit of the law rather than taking advantage of any loopholes it might have offered to permit dubious fills. In the commission's view, projects that met the two qualifica-

Edge of the Bay: Aquatic Park, Berkeley, saved by conservationists

tions of the law totaled 359 acres of fill over the three-year period. Of this, 75 acres were for an extension of a runway at Oakland Airport and 180 acres for a fill at San Francisco Airport. Most of the rest was for waterfront development for public access and recreation in San Leandro, Berkeley and San Mateo.

After 120 years, the unrestricted filling of San Francisco Bay had been brought to a halt.

101

29338

THERE is an incomparable day that comes once a year on the Bay. It arrives not according to any man-made calendar, but like the date of Easter is determined by what happens in the sky. Like Easter, too, it is a day of awakening, but it comes always in the fall of the year. It is the first clear day after the first rain.

Early autumn, like early spring, is the time of soft haze, of muted colors, of peace and somnolence. Then, perhaps without warning, the rains come. They may come in a series of showers or in a drenching downpour; they may last for a day or for a week; but their aftermath is the same.

One morning the rains are gone; the mists are washed away, and with a sudden crescendo the Bay is brilliant with new life. The wind is sharp and cold; the air sparkles; the Bay radiates with an intensity of light not seen since winter. The cliffs and rocks of the Golden Gate are fringed with white breakers, and the light glitters and dances across the cobalt surface flecked with whitecaps.

The great bridge at the strait, which for months has been a vague, floating outline in the fogs and mists and clouds, now leaps again from shore to shore with incredible intensity

103

and vividness, each of its harp-string cables, every chord
of its steel-webbed deck, every sculptured ridge of its sky-
reaching towers clear in the morning sun. A glint of light is
reflected from the windshield of a car on its deck, and answering flashes come from the deck of the Bay Bridge ten
miles across the water.

The entire Bay reflects the sharp invigorating radiance
of this superlative moment of the year. Around its shores
four million people are going to work, feeling in their pulses
the quickening splendor of this shining day.

— San Francisco Bay

12/ THE FUTURE OF THE BAY

It requires little imagination to picture the Bay region without the Bay. It is only necessary to look at many another U. S. city, surrounded by mile after mile of tract houses, asphalt-encircled shopping centers, factories and freeways — endless stretches of slurbs, choked by traffic, begrimed by smog. However, it requires considerable imagination, and a great deal of ingenuity, to picture this region if its greatest natural resource were preserved and developed to its fullest potential.

This kind of vision of what the Bay might become has been set forth by the Bay Conservation and Development Commission in the comprehensive plan it developed for the Bay and its shores. In this new vision of the future Bay, the whole magnificent body of water is still there, full-sized and more splendid than ever. It is no longer a neglected asset, bordered by garbage dumps and blighted, inaccessible waterfronts. It is a new source of beauty, recreation and scenic enjoyment for the four million people who live around its shores. Bay residents and visitors are able to encircle the shoreline on scenic drives with both panoramic and close-up views of the water; go boating at any of several dozen marinas; swim and water ski off new beaches, ride ferries connecting a series of major shoreline parks; go fishing from numerous beaches and piers; observe wildlife from walkways through the prolific marshlands; hike, bicycle or

From San Bruno Mountain: sunrise over the Bay 107

ride horseback on a trail system linking the parks; dine at restaurants overlooking both urban and natural waterfronts.

The San Francisco Bay Plan promised to be the Bay's Magna Charta, an affirmation of the Bay's right to exist, a declaration that this incomparable body of water would not be destroyed by filling, that it would be developed as a Bay, not as a source of real estate.

Much of the plan had been anticipated in the BCDC's 23 periodic reports on various aspects of the Bay. In addition to a statement of recommended policies to guide Bay and shoreline planning, the commission published a series of maps of all the Bay's shores illustrating how the policies could be applied.

The general principles of the plan were simple. Its goal was to protect and enhance the Bay by providing adequately for three main uses: as a harbor, as a center of water-related industry, as a prime recreational attraction — "a maximum of public benefits with a minimum of Bay filling." A limited amount of filling would be permitted for these purposes if it provided "substantial public benefits that are directly related to the Bay, if these same benefits could not be achieved equally well without filling."

Minor fills would be permitted "to improve the attractiveness of shoreline development, to make possible additional public access to the Bay, or to make possible additional recreational uses of the waterfront, if these improvements to shoreline development could not be achieved without filling."

The plan was quite clear that fills would be limited to these purposes because filling was potentially destructive to fish and wildlife habitat, as well as to the scenic beauty of the Bay, and would increase the danger of air pollution, water pollution and deterioration of the climate.

Following are the plan's major recommendations concerning bay and shoreline development. (A plan map and a detailed summary appear in the Appendix.)

TIDELANDS AND OPEN WATERS. ". . . To the greatest extent feasible, the remaining marshes and mudflats around the Bay, the remaining water volume and surface area of the Bay, and fresh water inflow into the Bay should be maintained."

PERMISSIBLE FILLS. High-priority uses of the shorelines — water-related recreation, ports, airports and water-related industry — would provide substantial public benefits and would consequently justify limited filling where necessary. Some filling would also be allowed for "Bay-oriented commercial recreation and water-related assembly purposes," such as restaurants, specialty shops and hotels, when the developer would also provide substantial public recreation and Bay access as part of his project.

RECREATION. Some 65 miles of the Bay's 276 miles of shoreline should be reserved for public recreation — marinas, launching ramps, swimming beaches and fishing piers, In addition, privately built marinas, ramps and piers should be encouraged, and recreational facilities should be incorporated into shoreline developments for ports, airports and industries.

PORTS. Expansion of existing ports and construction of new ports will be important to the economy of the Bay Area and will require some filling. Future port development should be guided by a regional port plan to avoid needless duplication of facilities and to minimize the fill needed.

AIRPORTS. To enable the Bay Area to have adequate airport facilities and to minimize the need for airport filling, there should be a regional airport plan, covering alternatives such as new small airports for middle-length trips and a new major airport inland. Existing airports on the Bay's shores can include airport-related industries, but no further filling should be permitted for this purpose.

INDUSTRY. Some 19,000 acres of shoreline land should be reserved for industries directly dependent on shipping. The use of this land should be carefully planned to minimize the length of shoreline needed, to allow public access to the Bay, and to make the waterfront esthetically attractive.

OTHER SHORELINE USES. Areas reserved for high-priority Bay-related uses (recreation, ports, airports and industry) would occupy only about half of the Bay's shoreline. The remainder could be used for any purpose that was not detrimental to the Bay and adjacent areas, at the option of the owner and the local government.

HOUSING. Residential developments would be permissible in non-priority shoreline areas, although no filling would be permitted for this purpose. Wherever possible in new residential developments, waterfront areas should be expanded by dredging new channels inland.

SAFETY. A Fill Review Board, consisting of experts in earth sciences and structural engineering, would be appointed to review all fill projects for hazards involved in long-run settling of the fill, faulty filling methods and earth-quakes.

DIKED PONDS. The Bay's 96,000 acres of salt ponds and diked hunting preserves are important to the ecology and climate and should be maintained as long as economically possible. If maintenance of the ponds becomes economically infeasible, the public should make every effort to buy them, breach the dikes and restore them to the Bay.

TRANSPORTATION. To reduce the need for new

bridges and highways on the Bay, transportation planning should emphasize the use of tunnels and alternatives to automobiles, such as barges and passenger ferries.

PUBLIC ACCESS. Every new waterfront project should provide maximum public access to the Bay, and all permitted fills should result in increased accessible shorelines.

ENFORCEMENT. A limited regional government should be created to carry out the Bay Plan and other regional responsibilities. Its jurisdiction should include the Bay and limited shoreline areas in the nine Bay counties. If no such regional government is created, the Bay Plan should be carried out by a special Bay agency.

This, in outline, is the BCDC's San Francisco Bay Plan, first published in preliminary form in June of 1968. Some developers and other critics protested that the plan did not safeguard the rights of Bay property owners, allotted insufficient shoreline space for industry and placed too much emphasis on wildlife and ecology. When the commission in September revised the plan to permit filling for "Bay-oriented commercial recreation and water-related public assembly purposes," it was criticized by some conservationists as opening the door to fills for a wide range of commercial projects and violating the principle that there should be no filling except for essential purposes.

Doubtless these matters would be debated fully when the plan was presented to the 1969 Legislature. During the same session the Legislature was scheduled to hear the report of its Joint Committee on Bay Area Regional Organization (BARO), which was expected to recommend a regional government similar to that proposed by the BCDC. After generations of political fragmentation and destructive exploitation of the Bay, there was at last a unified plan.

Fort Mason, San Francisco; Alcatraz beyond

13 / THE NEW CONSERVATION

THE gradual destruction of San Francisco Bay by filling is the kind of phenomenon that is familiar to Americans acquainted with the history of their country. As Stewart L. Udall has pointed out in *The Quiet Crisis,* a century ago it was common practice to exploit our natural resources for the last dollar that could be squeezed from them. The world's greatest forests were logged and burned over in a swath of destruction beginning in New England and proceeding down through New York and Pennsylvania, across to the lake states, over the Rockies and on to the Pacific coast where the giant redwoods were logged indiscriminately with scant regard for the fact that they were the supreme climax of the continent's plant life.

The wildlife was hunted to the brink of extermination — the beaver and seals and sea otter for their pelts, the egrets and herons for their feathers, the buffalo for hides and sport; and whole species, such as the passenger pigeon, were utterly destroyed.

The soils of the Great Plains, some of the most fertile on earth, were overgrazed and overplowed and laid bare to the elements until the winds and rains eroded vast areas into dust bowls as barren as the surface of the moon.

The minerals in the earth were despoiled by reckless mining; millions of barrels of oil were allowed to spew into the air, flow into streams, or were carelessly set afire in an unparalleled orgy of waste.

The entire nation from ocean to ocean would doubtless have been denuded of its resources and future generations would have inherited a land as sterile as some of the lifeless eroded regions of the Middle East — had not a few farsighted individuals called the nation to its senses.

John Muir, Gifford Pinchot, and Theodore Roosevelt began the conservation movement, and it came in the nick of time to salvage what was left of our natural resources and put brakes on the runaway exploitation that was destroying the common wealth for private profit.

The philosophy of conservation was based on the premise that the natural resources of the continent are not the property of the present generation to destroy or despoil; they belong to all future generations and must be used in ways that will safeguard the rights of our descendants.

Much progress has been made in the conservation of our commercial resources — forests and minerals and farmland and wildlife. Much remains to be done in these fields. But today conservation is moving into a new area and takes on expanded meanings. It is beginning to be concerned not simply with commercial resources but with environmental resources as well. Air, rivers, streams, beaches, lakes, bays, scenic and recreational open space are resources that are becoming as valuable to our increasingly crowded urban culture as timber, soil, wildlife, and minerals. And as urbanization increases they are increasingly exploited and despoiled for private profit. Air breathed by millions is besmogged; water for drinking, recreation, and esthetic enjoyment is polluted by refuse or filled in for expansion of subdivisions, highways, and industrial sites.

This kind of destruction, if uncurbed, will leave future generations with an eroded environment, begrimed, dreary, polluted, and as hostile to physical and mental health as lands which have been stripped of their forests and wild-life, minerals and soil.

Today new John Muirs, Gifford Pinchots, and Theodore Roosevelts are leading a crusade for environmental conservation, and the effort to save San Francisco Bay is representative of what is happening across the land. The new conservationists are confronting some of the same obstacles and arguments faced by their predecessors around the turn of the century: you can't interfere with private enterprise; land belongs to the owner and he can do with it as he pleases; you can't stop progress. This has been the kind of reasoning used historically to justify the most merciless exploitation and destruction of natural resources.

The answer, of course, is that the nation has long since decided that it does have the right to restrict the use of resources on which the national community, present and future, must depend. As a natural resource, San Francisco Bay eminently qualifies for the same kind of protection.

Perhaps the most difficult task of the contemporary conservationists is to dispel the common assumption that the supreme goal of every community is to "grow," to compete in the population sweepstakes, to add as many people as possible, to expand in every direction, across the land and into the water.

Advocates of the philosophy that "bigger" and "better" are synonymous need to be reminded that there are different kinds of growth. The healthy child wants to grow in size; the healthy adult prefers to grow in quality. For the adult, continued growth in size is pathological. It is time our communities entered municipal adulthood and began to place quality above quantity, health above disease.

The San Francisco Bay Area, like many other U. S. urban centers, must choose between unlimited growth in size and planned growth in the quality of living in all aspects — recreational, educational, esthetic, cultural. It is doubtless possible from an engineering standpoint to fill the entire Bay, except for the ship channels, with subdivisions, factories, freeways and parking lots. In the words of Wallace Stegner, the Bay is on its way to being converted into ''a fuming flat with a sewage canal down its center, a region of pollution, crowding and ugliness.''

However if the Save-the-Bay movement is successful, this vast estuary can be not merely preserved but enhanced and developed as the common center of a spectacular water-oriented community, taking full advantage of this incomparable combination of cities, and mountains and waters.

As anticipated in the BCDC plan, the potential uses of the Bay include not only recreation and industry but agriculture and transportation. It may well become important to ''farm'' the Bay's waters by raising oysters and other shellfish, developing new fisheries and harvesting an algae crop for conversion into food. Full advantage should be taken of the Bay's surface for transportation between the shoreline cities. Rather than covering the Bay with a network of bridges and freeways, it would be desirable to make use of a wide range of water craft, which could be at least as efficient as automobile transportation and far more enjoyable. Ferries could carry masses of commuters across the Bay between shoreline rapid transit stations; jet-propelled speed-

116

Modes of Bay travel: hydrofoil

boats, hydrofoils or hovercraft could operate on fast sched-
ules along the shore between San Francisco and other cities
from San Jose to Petaluma to Sacramento.

Waterfront parks, with boating facilities, picnic sites,
beaches and overnight hostels, could be linked with ferries
and connected with green belts extending through the cities
to regional parks back in the mountains. Unprecedented
new recreational possibilities would be opened up by the
opportunity to hike, cycle or ride horseback through parkways entirely around the Bay. On-the-spot museums and ex-
hibit centers could interpret the natural and man-made fea-
tures of the landscape and the cityscape. The educational
possibilities are unlimited, and the scenic splendor arising
from the planned development of this unparalleled environment would attract visitors from around the world.

117

Pt. Pinole

14 / BAY OF DESTINY

For 200 years the promise of this Bay has been manifest in diverse ways to the explorers, the pioneers, the gold-seekers, the empire-builders, the latter-day immigrants. Padre Pedro Font, chaplain of the Anza expedition in 1776, described the Bay as "a prodigy of nature . . . the harbor of harbors."

The venturesome Russian Nicolai Rezanov in 1806 wrote to his superiors in St. Petersburg that this superb Bay and its shores should become part of the Russian empire. Richard Henry Dana in 1835 predicted that "this magnificent Bay, . . . the best anchoring grounds in the whole western coast of America," would become the center of a prosperous commonwealth. John C. Fremont in 1846 compared the Bay region with the ancient imperial capital of Byzantium, crossroads between Europe and Asia, and recalling that the entrance to the harbor of Byzantium was called Chrysoceras, or Golden Horn, prophetically named this entrance Chrysopylae — Golden Gate. The Forty-Niners who arrived by ship saw this body of water as the avenue to opportunity, symbol of their visions of wealth and glory. Their dream, with variations, has been shared by millions who have since come to live on these shores.

Certainly the possibilities of the Bay as the center of a regional metropolis include its role as one of the economic capitals of the Western world, facing across this ocean the burgeoning lands of Asia — in the words of Richard Henry Dana, the "emporium of a new world, the awakened Pacific." But its potential lies also in the opportunities it affords for the evolution of new patterns of living in the coming age of leisure, for felicitous combinations of business and recreation around the water, for the development of a new kind of metropolitan region in which man's relation to his natural environment is not exploitive but creative.

If the present uses of the Bay as real estate, as a sewer and as a garbage dump can be halted permanently and replaced by imaginative planning, it may be possible to develop here new ways of water-oriented living in a metropolitan community as different from the conventional American urban region as the city of Venice was different from the old introverted walled towns of medieval times. For such a community, the Bay Plan, if boldly strengthened and enforced, can provide both the vision and the initial charter.

But a plan is nothing more than an opportunity, an instrument, a means to an end. Whether this plan is effectively used and expanded — whether the potential water-oriented metropolis comes into being on these shores — will depend on the quality of the people who administer the plan, on the continued vigilance of those dedicated citizens who have worked unceasingly to halt the filling, and on the degree to which residents of the region grasp the high promise and historic destiny of San Francisco Bay.

Point Pinole, Richmond, site of planned Bethlehem Steel plant expansion

IT has been said that all great cities of history have been built on bodies of water — Rome on the Tiber, Paris on the Seine, London on the Thames, New York on the Hudson. If this is a criterion of a city's greatness, surely San Franrisco ranks in the first magnitude among cities of the world. For never was a metropolis more dominated by any natural feature than San Francisco by its Bay.

In Rome, Paris, London, New York, once away from the water's edge you quickly lose track of it in the buzzing swarm of the city's interior. But San Francisco lies at the tip of a peninsula, and anywhere within the city's forty-five square miles a view of the water is only a few steps away at most — to the head of the block or the roof of the building or the top of the hill.

East of the peninsula's central ridges the city slants toward the Bay. All of the downtown district and the older residential areas lie within the valleys and hills of this eastward slope. The salt fragrance penetrates every neighborhood. The bass drones of the foghorns and the whistles of ships are as common as the sound of automobile horns in the streets.

You can climb Twin Peaks and see several hundred square miles of Bay spread around you like a glowing tapestry of light and color. More often the Bay's impact comes unexpectedly. Rounding a corner in the heart of the city, you see it suddenly in the distance between nearby houses, blue in the sun. Waiting for an elevator in a downtown building, you glance out the window and are startled to see a high swinging arc of the Bay Bridge.

The Bay seems always around you. It shines in the distance beyond the long rows of bulging bay-windowed flats. It appears at the bottom of the streets that drop dizzily down from the city's heights. It glows beyond the narrow, cluttered alleys of Chinatown.

It is before you as you drive over a rise of Russian Hill and see its sudden gleam and sparkle between nearby trees. It comes to you in a series of brief, breath-taking views, as you rise on the Powell cable car over Nob Hill and get successive glimpses of it at the ends of the cross streets — a shining shield of blue spanned by the giant bridge arching across the water to the cities and hills of the far shore.

— San Francisco Bay

APPENDIX 1/ THE SAN FRANCISCO BAY PLAN

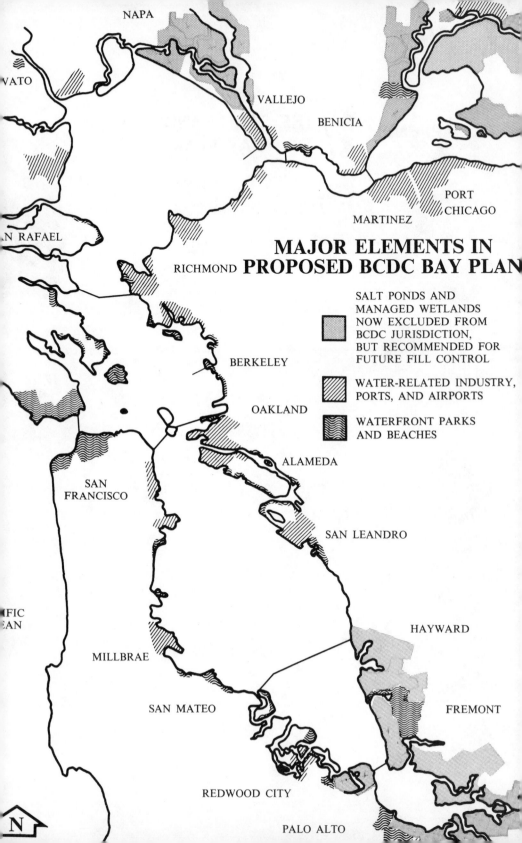

MAJOR ELEMENTS IN PROPOSED BCDC BAY PLAN

Legend:

- SALT PONDS AND MANAGED WETLANDS NOW EXCLUDED FROM BCDC JURISDICTION, BUT RECOMMENDED FOR FUTURE FILL CONTROL
- WATER-RELATED INDUSTRY, PORTS, AND AIRPORTS
- WATERFRONT PARKS AND BEACHES

NAPA
VALLEJO
BENICIA
PORT CHICAGO
MARTINEZ
SAN RAFAEL
RICHMOND
NOVATO
BERKELEY
OAKLAND
ALAMEDA
SAN LEANDRO
SAN FRANCISCO
HAYWARD
MILLBRAE
SAN MATEO
FREMONT
REDWOOD CITY
PALO ALTO
PACIFIC OCEAN

N

A SUMMARY

In keeping with its responsibilities for both conservation and development, the BCDC's findings and policies were presented in two parts corresponding with its two basic goals: "Protection of the Bay as a great natural resource for the benefit of present and future generations and development of the Bay and its shoreline to their highest potential with a minimum of Bay filling."

Following is a summary of the BCDC's findings and recommendations on conservation matters:

FISH AND WILDLIFE: In order to maximize human benefits from fish and wildlife, including food, economic gain, recreation, scientific research, education, and a high-quality environment, it is necessary to maintain sufficient oxygen in the water, adequate food, sufficient shelter space, and proper water temperature, salt content, and velocity of the currents. The plan recognized the key role of marshes and mudflats in the Bay's chain of life. These are precisely the areas that would be occupied by most fill projects.

". . . To the greatest extent feasible," the plan recommended, "the remaining marshes and mudflats around the Bay, the remaining water volume and surface area of the Bay, and fresh water inflow into the Bay should be maintained."

WATER POLLUTION: Recent improvements in sewage disposal have reduced pollution generally, but some areas of the Bay are still badly polluted at certain times of the year. Consequently improvements in waste treatment are essential. It is recognized, however, that the Bay will continue to receive some liquid wastes. To handle these wastes it is necessary to insure adequate flushing by tidal movements and sufficient supply of the dissolved oxygen which is essential to natural breakdown of sewage.

Fills of any kind diminish the volume of water flowing in and out on the tides and usually eliminate tidal flats and shallow areas, which have the largest oxygen-producing capacity. Here, then, is another reason to maintain the remaining marshes and mudflats, as well as maximum water volume and surface area. The cleansing function of these shallows is essential to attain the plan's goal: water quality permitting swimming and other water contact sports in all parts of the Bay.

SMOG AND WEATHER: Because substantial filling would diminish air circulation, raise summer temperatures in certain areas and increase both fog and smog, the present volume and surface area of the Bay should be maintained to the greatest extent feasible.

BAY BARRIERS: Although some proposals for dams or barriers in the Bay would increase water circulation, they are not recommended because of their adverse effects on the Bay's appearance and ecology, sedimentation, flood control and various present and potential shoreline uses.

MARSHES AND MUDFLATS: Owing to their benefits in wildlife and marine life habitats, and in controlling water pollution, marshes and mudflats should not only be preserved as far as possible but should be augmented: former marshes that have been diked off can be restored by breaching the dikes; new marshes can be created by strategic placement of mud dredged from the Bay bottom for shipping channels and other purposes.

FRESH WATER INFLOW: Fresh water from tributaries, particularly the Sacramento-San Joaquin Delta, carries more dissolved oxygen than does salt water, helping dissipate wastes, and flushes out the northern part of the Bay during heavy runoffs. Mingling gradually with the salt water of the Bay, it provides a transition zone essential to migrating fish, particularly salmon and striped bass. The California Water Plan, by taking out water upstream, might diminish this fresh water flow into the Bay by as much as 80 per cent. Potential damage to the oxygen content and flushing of the Bay should be carefully evaluated and corrective measures taken.

DREDGING: Mud dredged from the Bay bottom to maintain shipping channels and harbors is usually dumped elsewhere in the Bay. Most of it is recirculated within the Bay by the tidal currents and may have to be dredged again. To break this vicious circle, "mud from future dredging should be: (1) placed on dry land, (2) used as a source of fill for approved fill projects, (3) taken out to sea by barge or pipeline to suitable disposal sites, or, if no other alternative is available, (4) dumped in designated parts of the Bay where the maximum possible amount will be carried out the Golden Gate on the ebb tides."

To reduce the amount of sediment reaching the Bay from tributaries, "the Bay agency should encourage increased efforts by soil conservation districts and public works agencies in the 50,000-square-mile tributary area to continuously reduce soil erosion as much as possible." To protect natural fresh water reservoirs beneath the Bay floor, all proposals for deep dredging or construction should require approval of the State Department of Water Resources.

SHELL DEPOSITS: Oyster shells from the Bay bottom provide a valuable source of lime used in the production of cement. To preserve this natural resource, fills that adversely affect shell deposits should be prohibited except for purposes providing greater public benefit than the shells.

The recommendations of the Bay Plan in the field of conservation are supplemented by the recommendations for development, summarized as follows:

ECONOMIC AND POPULATION GROWTH: Population projections for the Bay Area indicate that the number of residents will grow from 4.5 million in 1967 to 6.2 million in 1980, 7.6 million in 1990 and 10.8 million in 2020.

SAFETY OF FILLS: Building on fills which rest on the soft mud of the Bay bottom might be affected by gradual settling or by sudden collapse owing to either faulty filling or sharp earthquakes.

A Fill Review Board should be appointed to develop fill construction standards, to review all fill proposals and to inspect fills during construction. Even though otherwise permissible, no fill or building should be constructed if it cannot meet these standards. To provide data on any soil movements, seismographs should be placed on all major fills and in other crucial areas.

WATER-RELATED INDUSTRY: Many industries are dependent on shipping of raw materials or finished products. Land suitable for these industries will probably be in short supply within the next 50 years and thus should be reserved now for these uses. On the basis of 50-year manufacturing employment estimates, the Bay plan designates 19,000 acres for waterfront to be reserved for water-related industry (in addition to the 6000 already in this use).

Interim uses may be permitted on this land until it is needed for water-related industrial purposes. In order to economize the use of this land, storage and waste treatment ponds on the shoreline should be avoided; dock facilities should be shared where possible; the longest dimension of plants should be at right angles rather than parallel to the shoreline; and new highways or rail lines should be away from the waterfront.

Waterfront industrial facilities should be made as attractive as possible by compliance with highest feasible air and water pollution standards, by terracing rather than leveling any Bayfront hills, by preserving public overlook points and historic sites, by maximizing public access to the shoreline. These practices should be encouraged by tax benefits and other incentives.

A regional planning program should study all possible industrial sites in the region and perhaps reserve inland industrial sites for industries not requiring water frontage. Such a program would take pressure off the shoreline.

PORTS: Although shipping is vital to the Bay Area economy, there is no coordinated planning and development of the Bay's ports. Various terminals use Bay fill and shoreline areas for unnecessarily duplicating and competing port uses. Consequently there should be a regional port development plan which would minimize filling and possibly a regional agency to finance or develop certain facilities. The Bay plan as indicated on the maps would accommodate estimated port requirements to the year 2020 with a minimum of filling.

AIRPORTS: The rapid expansion of air traffic will create additional pressure for Bay fill to enlarge shoreline airports. To meet growing aviation needs and minimize filling, a regional agency should prepare a plan for a regional airport system. Pending completion of the plan, some short-range air traffic (such as San Francisco-Los Angeles flights) should be diverted to smaller airports, such as those in San Jose, Santa Rosa and Napa. Filling and construction for major airports should be limited to whatever is needed before 1979, by which time the regional airport system should be in operation. Expansion or construction of new general aviation facilities should be inland, and not on new Bay fill, unless no feasible alternative is available. Airports on and around the Bay may include airport-oriented industries (those using air transportation for the movement of goods and personnel or providing services to airport users) if these facilities cannot feasibly be located elsewhere, but no fill should be permitted for such industries.

A regional agency might be required to finance or develop airport facilities inland to relieve pressure on the Bay for airport fills.

SALT PONDS AND OTHER DIKED WETLANDS: On the margins of the Bay there are 46,000 acres of salt ponds (owned by the Leslie Salt Company) and 50,000 acres of duck hunting preserves — all former tidal marshes now diked off from the Bay. The salt is an important natural resource for Bay Area industry, and all the diked areas are important to wildlife and climate. Consequently the salt ponds and hunting preserves should be maintained as water areas, and property taxes on them should be low. Recreational facilities, such as marinas, fishing piers, bathing beaches should be developed on the outer side of the dikes.

If owners of these diked areas decide to withdraw any ponds from their present uses (by 1969 some 4500 acres of salt ponds had been filled for urbanization) "the public should make every effort to buy these lands, breach the

136

existing dikes, and reopen these areas to the Bay.'' Meantime, the public might purchase development rights; in effect the owners would be compensated for giving up the right to fill the ponds for subdivisions or other uses. If public purchase of the land or development rights is not feasible and the ponds are filled, substantial portions should remain as open water.

WATERFRONT PARKS, MARINAS AND FISHING PIERS: Only about 15 or so of the 276 miles of Bay shore are in waterfront parks. Recreation demands are increasing faster far more rapidly than the population. Consequently if sufficient recreational land is not reserved now for the next 50 years, potential park lands will be rapidly preempted by other uses. Based on the projected population of 10.8 million in the year 2020, about 65 miles of shoreline will be required for marinas, launching ramps and swimming beaches.

The Bay plan maps provide that land should be reserved for 78 marinas and 26 fishing piers. These will not be adequate for the 50-year demand, however, and other privately-built marinas, piers and launching ramps should be permitted provided they would not interfere with other priority uses. Besides specific recreation areas, efforts should be made to integrate some recreational facilities into ports water-related industries and airports. Some of the new beaches should be developed next to plants discharging warm water. All varieties of commercial water-oriented recreation developments should be encouraged in urban areas, and these facilities should be linked by a fleet of small inexpensive ferries similar to those that operate on some European lakes and rivers. Shoreside parks should provide some camping areas accessible only by boat, as well as trails for hiking, bicycling, and horseback riding, picnic areas, viewpoints, beaches and fishing facilities.

SCENIC VIEWS: To take full advantage of the dramatic view potential from the hills and shoreline, Bay front buildings should be clustered to leave view areas open; vista points should be provided (as indicated on the plan maps); interpretive exhibits should be provided; scenic parkways should be encouraged; and bridges should be designed to permit maximum outlooks.

OTHER SHORELINE USES: Priority uses described above would require only about half the Bay's shoreline. The undeveloped portion of the remainder could be used for any purpose that treats the Bay as an asset to its development. Among these purposes would be water-oriented commercial recreation available to the public, such as beaches, restaurants, specialty shops and hotels. Limited filling would be permitted for these purposes provided no public agency had planned projects on the site affording adequate Bay access, a substantial portion of the new shoreline were permanently open to the public free of charge and without the expenditure of public funds, a substantial portion of the project were built on existing land, fish and wildlife habitat were enhanced as far as possible, and the project established a permanent new shoreline by precluding all further offshore filling.

For more private shoreline uses such as housing no filling would be permitted, and wherever possible waterfront areas should be expanded by dredging new channels inland.

High population densities should be encouraged to provide waterfront advantages to maximum numbers of people. Houseboat colonies may be permitted along the shore where they cause no damage to other Bay values.

Utility lines along the shore should be underground wherever feasible; elsewhere they should be placed and designed for minimum esthetic damage.

Owing to the pressure to use the Bay for freeways, transportation planning should reduce dependence on the automobile as far as possible and rely on new systems of transit, such as fast barges (for truck and freight transport) and modern ferry systems both across the Bay and parallel to its shores for business and pleasure use. San Francisco might have water links not only with Oakland and Sausalito but also with Palo Alto and San Jose, Richmond, San Rafael and Vallejo, possibly even Stockton and Sacramento.

Before any additional freeways or bridges are approved for the Bay, there should be intensive research and testing to determine whether tunneling or other methods of transportation could achieve the same purpose. If approved, freeways and bridge approaches should be built on piles rather than fills, should provide clearance for all water craft, and should provide for mass transit facilities.

Refuse disposal should not be permitted in shore areas unless it is suitable for an approved fill. Junkyards and dilapidated structures shoud be banned entirely.

APPEARANCE AND DESIGN OF SHORELINE DEVELOPMENTS: To enhance the appearance of the shores, all waterfront construction and other developments should be planned with participation by such professionals as landscape architects, urban designers or architects as well as engineers. A Design Review Board should develop criteria and give advisory opinions on the appearance of all projects affecting waterfronts.

PUBLIC ACCESS: In addition to the public access to the Bay to be provided by shoreline parks and recreational developments, every new waterfront project of any kind should provide maximum access for pedestrians. Permitted fills should result in an increase in the amount of accessible Bay frontage. Shoreline roads should be scenic parkways principally for slow-moving recreational travel (not for through traffic) and should provide for safe pedestrian access to the shore. All shoreline parks and access points should be linked by scenic drives, trails or inland waterways.

This, then, was the BCDC's San Francisco Bay Plan. Its goal was to maintain and improve the Bay and its shoreline to enrich the quality of life in the San Francisco Bay Area. The plan in its preliminary form was called by Leslie Carbert, former State Planning Offiicer, "one of the most exciting and unique planning documents in modern Americana."

APPENDIX 2 / CARRYING OUT THE PLAN

Every plan needs "teeth." Without a means of implementation, it will amount to little more than fanciful designs on paper. The McAteer-Petris Act directed the commission to prepare "a comprehensive and *enforceable* plan for the conservation of the water of San Francisco Bay and the development of its shoreline."

After making its report to the 1969 Legislature, the BCDC was to go out of existence 90 days following adjournment. Its recommendations would obviously have to include a successor organization to enforce the plan.

Here the BCDC's recommendations began to reach far beyond the Bay itself. From one viewpoint they would result in major changes in the way the Bay Area was governed. Yet from another viewpoint they simply involved a logical extension of a process that had been taking place for many years.

It had long been obvious that the region had outgrown the governmental arrangements devised more than a century ago. None of the nine counties around the Bay was self-contained, and many local activities affected other parts of the Bay Area. The Bay itself was but one example of a resource that was vital to the entire region and could no longer be adequately dealt with by cities and counties alone. Just as sewage dumped into one part of the Bay could pollute the entire body of water, so smoke from one city or county could reduce air quality across many boundary lines. Similarly, transportation and waste disposal had long since become regional matters.

In response to the growth of these region-wide problems, there had been set up over a period of years a number of separate agencies with regional and sub-regional responsibilities, including the Bay Area Air Pollution Control District, the Regional Water Quality Control Board, the Bay Area Transportation Study Commission, the East Bay Regional Park System, the Association of Bay Area Governments, the Bay Area Rapid Transit District.

Rather than add one more separate agency to this long list of independent, uncoordinated and sometimes conflicting organizations, most of which had a direct impact on the Bay, the BCDC recommended that responsibility for the Bay plan be placed in a limited regional government or multi-purpose agency that presumably would embrace some or all of these individual agencies. Although the BCDC did not go into detail, it might be hoped that the agency would have regional responsibilities in other areas affecting the Bay, including both those covered by existing regional agencies and those not now the job of any regional agency, such as harbors, airports and solid waste. The recommended regional government would not replace local governments but would deal only with regional matters transcending their boundaries.

As second choice, the BCDC recommended a special agency to be concerned with the Bay alone, with provision for making it part of any future regional government.

142

APPENDIX 3 / THE COST OF SAVING THE BAY

Special problems in carrying out the San Francisco Bay Plan would arise in three areas. They would concern the plan's effect on the urban poor, on Bay property owners, and on the general taxpayer.

The Bay and the Ghetto

At a time when the single most urgent domestic issue in the United States is the plight of the poor, particularly ethnic minorities, any major metropolitan-area plan must be assessed for its impact on the inhabitants of the slums or ghettoes.

Obviously, every resident of the region, regardless of income or economic status, has a stake in clean air and water and a pleasant climate. In addition, it happens that a large number of the so-called ghetto districts are near the Bay's shores—at Hunters Point—Bayview in San Francisco; at Marin City; along the waterfronts of Oakland, Berkeley, Emeryville, Richmond; in East Palo Alto and Menlo Park.

From one point of view, it might seem that the residents of these areas would benefit if the Bay were filled for nearby industry to supply jobs. From a broader viewpoint, however, it is evident that this kind of development would tend

143

to perpetuate the ghetto. In the long run, the ghettoes can be dispersed only if employment opportunities are dispersed. There is ample vacant land elsewhere in the region for industrial expansion; less than one-fifth of the land in the nine counties is developed.

An efficient transportation system and provision for industrial employment and low-cost housing in the outer areas would tend to break up the ghetto pattern. The limited regional government proposed in the Bay Plan might well encourage this kind of balanced industrial and residential pattern as one of its principal functions. Meantime slum residents would benefit directly from the development of recreational facilities on nearby waterfronts — parks, fishing piers, swimming beaches. The horizons of children as well as adults would no longer be bounded by the walls of the ghetto but would extend to the Bay and its far shores, bringing beauty and recreational opportunities to the blighted areas. Certainly shoreline developments for these purposes should be given the most urgent priority by all agencies concerned with the Bay.

Owners of the Bay

The most difficult problem arising from the Bay Plan concerns the rights of property owners. Some 22% of the Bay floor is privately owned, and under the Bay Plan all but a small proportion of these areas would remain open and not subject to fill.

What could an owner of submerged lands or tide lands do with his property if he were denied a permit to fill? Some underwater property might be used for dredging oyster shells used in making cement, for commercial fishing piers or for "fish farming." But much Bay property would be of little value to the owner if filling were not permitted.

144

An obvious way out of this dilemma would be for the Bay agency to buy outright the 57,000 acres of privately owned Bay land. The price of such a large-scale purchase is difficult to estimate. Sales of Bay lands from 1960 through 1967 indicated prices extending on a vast range from about $150 an acre to about $22,000 an acre, depending on location. There were no figures on average prices, but if the average were $500 an acre, the total cost would be some $29 million. At an average price of $10,000 an acre, the cost of buying back the privately owned parts of the Bay would be $570 million.

The magnitude of these figures can be appreciated by comparing them with the size of the largest park bond issue ever passed by the voters of California — $150 million in 1964. This amount was for both state and local parks throughout California. There would obviously be serious difficulties in raising what might amount to several times that amount for similar purposes in the Bay Area alone, even though Federal grants might be available for some portion of the cost.

An alternative to buying the private lands on the Bay floor would be simply to deny owners permission to fill, paying them no compensation. Concerning the legality of this procedure, the BCDC report on "Powers" declared: "The traditional American rule of law has been that . . . regulation so strict as to deprive the owner of any economic use of his land is a 'taking' of his property. The owner may bring a lawsuit either to invalidate the regulation or to force the regulating body to compensate him . . . But times are changing, and the law has changed . . . According to one of the nation's foremost experts on the law of public land use regulation, the courts would probably uphold a statute declaring that privately owned lands in San Francisco Bay could not be filled — and that owners were not entitled to compensation for being refused permission to fill.''*

Another legal basis cited by the BCDC for denying permission to fill is the ''public trust for commerce, fishing, and navigation.'' Under this trust, derived from English common law and enacted into State law, ''the public originally had a right to use all tide and submerged lands in the Bay for commerce, fishing and navigation, and retains that right even over lands in private ownership unless the right was cut off with legislative approval. The public trust with regard to some parts of the Bay has been terminated by action of the Legislature, but the trust unquestionably still applies to many thousands of privately owned acres in the Bay.''

In the public trust areas, filling for most purposes could be legally prevented, although determining which lands are covered by the trust might be a complicated matter.

Even if the courts were to decide that owners could legally be denied the right to fill without compensation, there would still be the question of fairness and justice. An owner who bought Bay land in good faith and paid taxes on it with the intention of filling or selling at a profit could argue that he is morally entitled to compensation if he is refused permission to fill — at least to the amount of his investment. On the other hand it can be argued that any property purchase on a speculative basis necessarily involves risks and that the public is not obliged to reward land speculation.

---

* ''For the courts to sustain such a regulation regarding the Bay, two conditions would have to be met: (a) The regulation would have to be based on evidence showing that such stringent restrictions were necessary. Presumably the studies made by the BCDC and other agencies would amply demonstrate the harmful effect of Bay filling. (b) The regulation allowing some property to be filled and prohibiting the filling of other property in the Bay would have to be based on an approved Bay plan that adequately explained the reasons for the differing treatment.''

It might also be argued that if an owner were to be protected against *losses* resulting from public actions (such as denial of a fill application), he would have no right to claim *gains* resulting from public actions. Most Bay-bottom land becomes valuable only as a result of public actions, including urban growth and the construction of roads and other facilities. In denying the right to fill, then, the public would only be denying the owner the right to take a profit on value which the public itself had created.

These are difficult problems involving the reconciliation of private rights with the public interest, and it is probably not possible or necessary to solve them completely in order to work out a system for regulating Bay filling. Besides the two alternatives we have been considering — public purchase of private Bay lands or denial of the right to fill without compensation — there is a third possibility, involving a compromise of the first two.

If an owner applied for a fill project that was not in accord with the Bay plan (on land not affected by the public trust) the Bay agency could attempt to buy the land, through negotiation or, if necessary, eminent domain. If purchase were not feasible (for lack of funds or any other reason), the agency might permit a limited amount of fill — enough to allow the owner to receive some economic return on his property. In most cases owners of submerged lands are also owners of the adjacent shoreline, and shore development in accordance with the plan could well give the owner a fair return on his total investment with little or no filling.

Differing circumstances would require that appropriate solutions be worked out by the Bay agency in each instance, allowing the owner some economic benefit while observing the basic principles of the Bay Plan. An owner would always have the opportunity to appeal to the courts against any arbitrary decisions by the agency.

The Bay and the Taxpayer

A vital element in any plan, particularly one as far-reaching as the Bay Plan, is the financial question: ''Where is the money coming from?''

Obviously very substantial sums would be necessary if the Bay agency (or regional government) were to buy large areas of Bay floor. If minimal filling were to be permitted or all fills not conforming to the plan were to be denied without compensation, the funds required to put the plan into operation would be far less but still sizeable. Even if no Bay lands were purchased to prevent filling, money would still have to be raised for operating expenses and for purchase of some shoreline park areas. The source of operating funds would depend on the type of agency established. The BCDC calculated that a tax of one-half cent per $100 of assessed valuation in the nine-county Bay Area would produce approximately the $500,000 needed annually.

Recreational shoreline development by private enterprise should be encouraged by all means possible, but public funds would still have to be raised for public parks and recreational facilities. The Bay Plan maps show 5800 acres of new waterfront recreational land, priced at roughly $30 million to $50 million (subject to inflation). An estimated half of the needed lands would be purchased by federal, state and local governments. The rest would be acquired by the agency carrying out the plan, possibly with the help of federal and state matching grants. Also to be considered is the cost of purchasing some of the 96,000 acres of diked ponds (or of development rights to the ponds) if necessary to prevent their being filled.

The BCDC suggests the funds for these purposes be raised by regional bond issues, preferably requiring a simple majority vote for passage (rather than two-thirds) and providing repayment from sources other than the heavily overburdened property tax.

These other sources might include an income tax, a sales tax or a real-estate transfer tax. The latter tax or some similar levy would recover a large share of the rise in property values resulting from urban growth, publicly-built roads and schools, and other social causes. It would thus tap a vast reservoir of profits from land speculation and minimize the burden on the ordinary property owner or consumer.

A further effect of the Bay Plan on the taxpayer should be noted. The creation of a separate Bay agency comparable to the BCDC would result in one more addition to the plethora of separate regional agencies concerned with various matters including air pollution, water pollution, parks, harbors, airports, bridges, and transit. It would seem obviously more economic and less of a drain on the taxpayers' pocketbook to coordinate or merge these overlapping agencies into a single limited regional government concerned with all of these matters, plus such other fields as solid waste and open space.

There is one more reason for limited regional government as opposed to the creation of further separate agencies. With each agency oriented toward its single purpose only, irreconcilable conflicts would inevitably arise. Transportation, particularly freeways, bridges and transit lines would come into collision course with agencies set up to preserve parks, Bay or open space. Separate harbors and airports could insist on the need for further Bay fill for their own competing purposes, whereas coordinated development might require little or no fill. And it would make little sense for both a Bay agency and a regional park agency to be responsible for regional recreation.

If it is not feasible to set up a regional government immediately, a separate Bay agency could nevertheless be created and go to work in the interim, with provision for including it within a future regional government.

It is clear that not all problems connected with the Bay Plan could be solved in advance. The plan would have the defect — or virtue — of all pioneering enterprises in that it could not be crystallized at the inception but would have to be pragmatically developed, expanded, and adapted to meet unforeseen circumstances. The preservation and development of San Francisco Bay to its fullest potential will be a mammoth undertaking, continuously requiring new ways of thinking about the Bay as a resource, about its place in the social fabric, about the relation of man to his total environment.

THE PHOTOGRAPHERS

Diane Beeston

26 - Race off St. Francis; 126, 127 - View from Nob Hill; 128 - Russian Hill and The Gate.

Michael Bry

8 - The water; 21 - Arriving tanker; 21 - Passenger liner; 28 - Richmond dump; 40 - Bayside living in Tiburon and Sausalito; 42 - Fisherman at the Gate; 48 - Gull; 48 - White egret in Richardson's Bay; 49 - Gulls; 52 - White egret; 57 - Fish; 68 - From Telegraph Hill; 75 - Tule fog in Marin; 82 - Filling by The Golden Gate; 102 - From Tiburon; 105 - Storm.

Richard Conrat

6, 7 - The Bay from Marin; 16, 17 - San Pablo Bay; 17 - Marsh grass; 22 - Reflection; 22 - Masts; 23 - From Angel Island; 24 - From Brooks Island; 30 - Avocets in tideland; 36 - Whose Bay?; 39 - Yerba Buena Cove; 49 - Shorebirds awaiting the ebb; 54 - Salt pond; 64 - At Antioch; 96 - Berkeley fill; 106 - Sunrise; 112 - From Ft. Mason; 118 - Pt. Pinole; 121 - At Pt. Pinole.

Kathleen Hoover

45 - White Pelicans; 46 - Grebe's nest; 47 - Brown Pelicans, Blue heron; 50 - Mallards.

Tom Meyers

67 - Ebbtide; 125 - Sunset at Golden Gate.

Rondal Partridge

28 - Dump Here; 60, 61 - Garbage; 73 - Smog level at Berkeley, Smogmakers; 90, 91 - Fill at Albany; 101 - Berkeley Lagoon.

Lynn Vardeman

Cover; 14 - The Bridge at Ft. Point; 18 - From Tiburon; 19 - Sausalito waterfront; 20 - Fog outside the Gate; 28 - Fill at Tiburon; 70, 71 - Fog at Golden Gate; 104, 105 - View from Golden Gate; 122 - From Belvedere.

Other Contributors

BCDC - 138, Ferry landing
Bay Hydrofoils, Inc. - 117, Hydrofoil
Cry California - 86, Map of fill; 130 Map of BCDC plan
San Francisco Convention & Visitors Bureau - 94, 95 - Night on Bay; 124, Night view from Twin Peaks; 125, View from Hyde St.
San Francisco Chronicle - 76, 1906 Earthquake.